GW00645445

For dear Donald
Birthday Greetings
and very best Wishes
with much love
from Helen

The Second Man in Us

Maria Röschl-Lehrs

The Second Man in Us
The Forming of the Inner Man
Through Spiritual Training

Edited by
Ernst Lehrs

HENRY GOULDEN

© HENRY GOULDEN LIMITED 1977

Translation by Robert Kolben and Jesse Darrell
Original German title: *Vom zweiten Menschen in uns. Zur Gestaltung des inneren Menschen auf dem geistigen Schulungswege.*
Published for the School of Spiritual Science, The Goetheanum, Dornach.
Copyright 1972 by Philosophisch-Anthroposophischer Verlag, Dornach
Switzerland.

English edition published by Henry Goulden Ltd.,
East Grinstead, Sussex.

Distributed in North America by the St. George Book Service, Spring Valley,
New York, 10977, U.S.A.

Library of Congress Catalogue Card Number: 77–79732

I S B N 0 904822 07 9

Printed by Scolar Press Ltd., Ilkley, Yorkshire

Contents

The Frontispiece: Maria Röschl-Lehrs (1890–1969)

Preface

In the spring of 1924 Rudolf Steiner appointed Dr. Maria Röschl as leader of the 'Youth Section' at the Goetheanum in Dornach. The problems which met her in this position were quite new, in that an ever-increasing number of the younger generation was in urgent movement towards Anthroposophy like a veritable wave of spirit. Disappointed elsewhere in their search for a meaning to life, longingly, endlessly seeking, inwardly awake for all their forcefulness and vehemence of will, they were now putting their questions to the spiritual knowledge of man and demanding answers. They were hungry for the spirit, for a nourishment of the soul which the existing sciences had entirely failed to satisfy.

At the very outset Maria Röschl found herself faced with the fact that the kind of education usual today gives the youthful human being very little basis for an understanding of the development of man as seen by spiritual knowledge. A discussion of the problem with Rudolf Steiner resulted in the decision that she should develop a 'young people's anthroposophy'. The basic works of Anthroposophy written by Steiner in the first decades of our century are mostly beyond the scientific range which can fairly be expected of a young person between the ages of 17 and 20. What is needed alongside one's own study at this age is above all the opportunity to discuss the problems of knowledge in groups and seminars, and thus to awaken to one's own individual being.

What met Maria Röschl in these young people was an endless variety of questions which sprang one and all from the longing to know something about the 'man in man'. They were looking for the second, the spiritual man in man, and asking how to bring him to birth in themselves.

To create ever new answers to this question became her life's task, and these essays are the result of this all-embracing work and her deep experience of the spirit. They are now being published in her memory as first leader of the 'Young People's Section'. They will find readers among those who are open to the spiritual word which carries with it impulses that are able to deepen life and give it the shape it needs.

RUDOLF GROSSE
Dornach, October 1972

Introduction

The essays appearing in the following pages were written during the 1920s and 30s, after the author had been appointed by Rudolf Steiner to be leader of the Section at the Goetheanum in Dornach that was concerned with the spiritual strivings of younger people. Like myself, some of her friends turned to these essays again after her death in order to renew their experience of what she had once set down in writing. The actuality in them was so strongly felt that all were of the opinion they should now be made accessible to a wider readership in these later years of the century. And so it was that since I had been her close collaborator throughout the period in question, as well as in married partnership with her for the last three decades of her life, I took on the responsibility myself of seeing them through publication.

Maria Röschl (born 1890, died 1969) was of Polish origin on her mother's side, her father being an Austrian treasury-official in that part of Poland belonging at the time to Austria. It was there that she was born and passed the first years of her life. Thus Polish was her first mother-tongue, being spoken at home even after the family had moved to Austria. Here German then became for her a second mother- or (perhaps more exactly) father-tongue.

Maria Röschl was not given to speaking much about herself, but once in her later life—she and I at the time were teaching at Hawkwood College in England—she did draw the curtain back a little. She was replying to a young friend in Sweden who had taken the first opportunity after the war to write to her for her sixtieth birthday, and in her own letter back she said:

'Yes, indeed! Life is rich—over-rich even, considering the shortage of time and the breakneck speed one has to live at! And so many souls, too many for counting, belong to the personal circle within which my life is breathing: I would like at times to be able to stretch right around Mother Earth—yes, from Finland to Peru in the far

1

South and from Shanghai the whole way over to California—so as to let these friends feel, however gently and tenderly, that I think of them, that I live, I weave with them. I think that if such a feeling became really strong, really true and powerful, the soul would be softly loosened from the body and people would say: she has died.— You write of your need to unite Anthroposophy with Christianity. With me it has never been otherwise. I found my way to Christianity long before my anthroposophical days, and in consequence every-thing has since ranged itself slowly around it. In our work too it is no different. The only thing is that my Christianity is in no way bound up with a church. I am a regular heretic for Christ! . . . The priesthood of *Man* is the only one evident to me, and for this reason I am so thankful I met Rudolf Steiner.

'You have detected the Pole in me. Yes, that lives on within from those life-streams and lines of the Polish landscape with its many contrasting forms that gives its children away. Only till I was twenty was I a Pole, and then came Goethe and fetched me away on to wider levels of human existence. And to him I remained faithful. Only the spiritual Poland interested me. I think I may say that in some measure I have lived with its spirits, and in fact still do, including the occultist Towiański,* who passed his last thirty years quite forgotten in Solot-hurn. In my experience there are not many Poles with the wish to be spiritually more than Poles. For whole nights on end I used to dance with them in Vienna, an elite, you could say, of the younger Poles of those days. They were like trinkets left behind by the folk-soul and now waiting for connoisseurs to come along and appreciate their real value. I almost married into Poland in 1919, but the day came when the pitiless question opened wide before me like an abyss: Do you know why? And I knew not at all. And as I was unreservedly honest, I told this to myself and to him, and we parted as friends.

'It was in this way that I left Poland behind me. Yet I have always been aware that the West, including Germany, has of necessity meant a burial in me, an entombment as a sort of adaptation of what lives in me of Slavonic verve and fire. Since that time, with all its strength and in my innermost being, it has been devoted to the spiritual. Now it may well be that the deeper significance of the road I have travelled lies in this. May in this way the burial lead to a true resurrection!'

It was characteristic of Maria Röschl's personality that her life represented a path of spiritual schooling which never deviated. Just how clearly she already recognised this herself when still quite young may be seen from two of the diary-entries she made as a student of twenty-three in her sixth semester at university, the one shortly after midnight as the new year of 1914 was beginning, the other a few days later:

'The year just over brought me many, many new experiences; many sorrows, though joys as well: towards the outer world, a rigid calm. Will this year prove more fruitful? In the one just past I took a real step forward in spiritual development. My whole life hitherto seems to me to have been a waiting in stillness in order to make this step possible, a preparation. And now I would gladly go further along this path to knowledge, to understanding rather, to a kind of understanding of the great world-connections of which man in his suffering and striving is himself a tiny image. In this understanding may I move forward as far as possible and live my life not only receptively but actively as well.'

'Apart from Goethe, I have met nobody who could fire me as much as W. Dilthey.* An hour ago I took up a book of his for the first time in my life; it was *Experience and Poetry*—and the mere reading of the Introduction moved me so much that I am still trembling for joy throughout my whole body. The depth in his words! What was the full compass of this spirit's thought when he jotted down just a few short words? They sound almost meagre compared with the deep levels they stir up in the mind of the reader. There you have the art of expression! A little crumb from a rich, deep, joyfully positive personality. Why do I never meet such people in actual life?'

It was not to be long before destiny gave her the answer and opened the way to the fulfilment of the wish she had expressed in the earlier diary-entry.

At that time psycho-analysis, still comparatively a newcomer with its interpretation of dreams and dreaming, was arousing a great deal of interest among many circles in Vienna. Maria Röschl was well-versed in this realm, for she had herself long possessed the gift of significant dreaming, and in such a way that psycho-analysis could only appear to her as an excrescence. This determined her to devote the dissertation for her doctorate to a consideration of dream-consciousness. As is already clear from the diary-quotations above, her

encounter with Goethe in the course of her study of German literature had proved decisive; accordingly she took as her theme *Goethe
and the Dream*. The thorough study of Goethe's work and the consideration of his personality which now became necessary made it
obvious to her, as she expressed it, that he could not be understood
without occultism. So as to come to a surer footing in this domain,
she asked her bookseller to let her have some literature about it,
and amongst the books he sent her she found *Knowledge of the Higher
Worlds: How is it Achieved?*[1] A first reading of it decided her that
there was only one way for her to form a judgment about it, and that
was to take the advice given for awakening the spiritual faculties
slumbering, as it said, in every human being, and actually apply it
to herself. This she did, and soon came to results which convinced
her she had found a path of inner schooling which was healthy and
suitable for the present time. The rest of her life served for a con-
sistent, ever-further advance along it.

In the letter already quoted from she goes on to tell how after
taking leave of her Polish friend she continued on her way alone.
Then she came one day quite unexpectedly to think of an earlier
acquaintance, the mother of a school-friend, an unusually fine nature,
whom long before she had got to know a little more closely but had
since not given any thought to. She decided to look her up immediately. As became clear later on, this visit was the next step on her
destined way to Rudolf Steiner; for quite unawares she was betaking
herself to an anthroposophist. Moreover, on arrival she found
another visitor already there, a young man she had herself known in
her student-days and who now also was an anthroposophist. He had
escaped from imprisonment in Russia and had just arrived in Vienna.
He was delighted to hear that she herself meanwhile had met with
the work of Rudolf Steiner and made an active connection with it.
At his suggestion and through him she joined the Anthroposophical
Society in Vienna.

This was Karl Schubert, who not long after left Vienna to become
a teacher at the recently founded Waldorf School in Stuttgart. It was
due to him again that some time later she herself received an offer
from the school of a future work there. This reached her in January
1921, seven years almost to the day after she had made the notes we
have quoted from her diary. After a first informatory talk with
Rudolf Steiner in Stuttgart, she decided to give up her position in a

girls' high school and go and teach in the Waldorf School instead. Half a year later, when she was about to begin her new work, Rudolf Steiner had a further conversation with her; from then on she was able to regard him as her personal teacher.*

ERNST LEHRS
Eckwälden, 1972

Why does Man Today Need a New Relationship to Nature?

Anyone who is really awake to the conditions of existence on earth today can come to see that what separates him from a deeper perception of the phenomena around him is nothing but a peculiarity of his own consciousness. Since the eighteenth century man has believed that the depths of knowledge are beyond him, and has erected the dogma of the boundaries of knowledge in order to be able with his own self-approval to extend ever further the kind of enquiry he practises over the mere surface of things. But the surface stops at a certain depth, below which lies the level that bears actual life. Man today has already delved as far down as this and is now standing before the riddle of life.

We cannot live by only breathing out: the stream of air must be drawn in again. Similarly, it is also in the nature of man that he breathes out his quest for knowledge into the universe, only to draw it back again into his innermost life-centre. When the plants burgeon and bloom in the spring he surges out into growing Nature and his eyes awaken to the enigma of the countenance she turns towards him. The experience of autumnal decay, of approaching winter, shows him the way back again into himself: 'How is it with you now', he can find himself saying, 'you, who have lived with Nature all the summer, enjoying her life to the full? You begin to see that all she shows you is a veil that hides the living truth. All this life of hers is simply a weaving of pictures. How will you learn to read these pictures?'

Nature directs man back into his own depths. She teaches him not to regard himself in his world-investigation as a riddle already solved, taking himself for granted and just dreaming his way into the surrounding world.

The experience of autumn turns man's enquiry from the outer to the inner, away from Nature into his own self. He feels the need to re-examine his instrument of knowledge, which is after all his own self. Faced with the riddle of Nature, he has the quite distinct experience: 'Here is a gate into all that is great, sublime and mighty; I am myself a small part of it. I depend on it for my life, the riddle of my life is rooted in its superhuman realm of forces. Only my consciousness separates me from it and its creative powers. My thinking, as it works in me today, sets up an impenetrable wall between it and myself.' When he looks within, he cannot but see that this thinking of his, which above all other human activities gives him the consciousness of his own humanity, leaves him at least once every twenty-four hours. This consciousness with which he sets out to investigate the external world he cannot retain without interruption, he has to submit to its periodic extinction. He cannot do otherwise, for without sleep he cannot exist.

Sleep takes the instrument of enquiry out of man's weary hand; dreams weave around him experiences that mock at the strict schooling of his logic. Even so, everyone knows the salutary effect of this change of consciousness: the refreshment of sleep without which our life-powers would soon be spent, and the enlightenment of many a dream-vision. Certainly, most dreams are confused and simply prattle about past occurrences. But these days it is no longer possible to deny that there are dreams that yield glimpses into supersensible realities. There was once a time when man went to sleep when the sun set and woke up again when the sun rose; his sleep was part of the rhythm of Nature. Now he has freed himself of this rhythm. Nevertheless, each time the earth rotates about its axis he still has to stand at any rate once before that other gate that does not lead him out into the riddles of Nature, of what is around him but discloses a deep, dark passage leading into his own inner being. At this gate his vivid day-consciousness is extinguished like a lamp whose oil is spent, and he partakes of an experience that is the exact opposite of the daytime clarity of his thinking: a weaving of pictures in which a part of his own being expresses itself—now in disconcerting clarity, now in tangled confusion.

Was this picture-language always so confused? No, it was not. There were times in the evolution of humanity when this dream consciousness could be a source of sublime knowledge, of a knowledge that had a much greater range, in time and space, than the waking thoughts of the daytime. Ancient history, and even that of the later middle ages, gives us numerous examples of this, and the poets of the past sang about it. The modern sceptic likes to dismiss the dreams of an earlier humanity as recorded in history or poetry as pure fantasy. But today we see scientific attempts to decode dream phenomena as a means of understanding the unconscious soul; collections of dreams are compiled that clearly show that the dream even now can be a source of knowledge. We are faced with the fact that every one of us—for there is hardly anyone who cannot remember ever having had a dream—has experience of how there can reach into the thinking cognition that has learnt to master the material world an utterly different state of consciousness whose form of expression is *the picture*.

If we now seek to experience Nature in a new way, we come to realize that the moment we begin to ask questions about the essential forces behind natural events, these all take on the form of pictures which actively express something deeply hidden, something that our present daytime consciousness cannot grasp. To grasp it, however, is just what we must learn to do, otherwise in approaching the pictorial character of cosmic events, we are liable to fall into the kind of dreams we have every night. It is essential, however, to stay awake at this boundary! And this we can manage if, instead of letting the pictures carry us away, we strive with the forces of our consciousness to penetrate into their reality. We are in a position to attempt this, since the phenomenon we are concerned with is in no way foreign to our nature; the dreams we are familiar with in our own inner life make use also of the language of pictures. If, however, we wish to understand the cosmic pictures, we must first learn something about our inner picture-life, and to do this we must sharpen our inner attention.

We can then arrive at two distinct experiences. The threefold inner life of thinking, feeling and willing, and the living human body this inner life makes use of as a vessel while it is awake, are separated from each other at night; the living vessel and the soul and spirit inhabiting it now come into a different relationship. We are of course alive during sleep: we still breathe, our blood flows, and we go on digesting what we have eaten. But our perception of external events fades out, our thinking, feeling and willing make no use of the sleeping body as a tool. This soul and spirit in us now faces another way and has another sort of experience, of which it brings back into our waking memory reflections which are sometimes clear, sometimes confused and distorted, in the form of the dream.

Attentive observation of one's own dreams over a period of years can show what connection exists between these images and the knowledge gained when awake. It is relatively easy to recognize the images reflecting certain physical disturbances. Although the images due to the same physical condition may widely differ in content, they will always be the same in their dynamic quality. A man suddenly overcome by some heart-weakness during sleep may dream that the air is drifting away from around him in coloured, ever darkening waves until it abandons him altogether, whereupon the light disappears and he falls into a dark pit; or he may see a giant fist slowly crushing a little bird to death; these are different images for the same process.

One may also observe the recurrence of certain animals in one's dreams, and then of certain feelings within oneself on waking. And it is possible to detect that whenever such an inner experience sets in, a corresponding picture is dreamed. It thus becomes clear that certain aspects of physical or mental life that may very well be beyond one's waking range of mind come into view disguised in the picture-language of dreams. One can make the attempt to read it.

I am not trying to represent the dream as an accurate source of knowledge, but simply indicating how dreams may express our innermost being in a picture-script, sometimes distinctly and accurately, sometimes almost illegibly.

The other experience each one can come to is the change his dream-life undergoes when he begins to arrange his life in a spiritual way according to Rudolf Steiner's indications in his book *Knowledge of the Higher Worlds: How is it Achieved?*.[1] If we strengthen our soul-spirit nature in our waking-life, carrying into it the ego-qualities of control, calmness and self-confidence, and during it directing our attention to the spiritual side of things, then we shall see that our dreams lose their confused condition and gain in significance.

Both experiences relating to our dreams show that they are only the expression of something higher in us, something that is not bound up with our life-processes but withdraws from them during sleep. Our living body rests in bed while our soul and spirit undergo far-reaching experiences beyond the boundaries of consciousness, bringing back into our memory on waking the pictures which are a pale reflection of these experiences.

The picture-experience reveals itself in this way as the first stage in a striving for knowledge beyond the material world. The picture is not the reality itself, it is not the spiritually active force, but it carries the stamp of this, it is its expression. This stamp may take various forms—no two artists after all will paint the same picture of the same scene. For the active spirit the picture is expression, not reality, and for the cognitive spirit the pictures becomes the means, not the object of knowledge; a means of knowledge all the same that is already free of physical appearance and flows over towards higher realms of knowledge.

The picture used to be the language of man's experience before he developed abstract thought: the ancient writings so full of wisdom, the oldest religious documents abound in pictures. Not yet able to grasp abstract thoughts, ancient man was shaped in his soul and spirit by the pictures of the myths that held sway within him. They guided him; they guided him along the path that in the end brought him to the development of that kind of thinking which now allows him his understanding and control of the material world. Just two such pictures may be mentioned here: the picture of Paradise with the tree of knowledge and the tree of life, and that of Prometheus chained to the rock while an eagle devours his liver. These pictures contain the most profound knowledge about the character of humanity and the path ordained for it.

The picture must become our means of expression again, if in the strength of our ego and the clarity of our consciousness we aim, as aim we must, at expanding our range of knowledge beyond the boundaries of abstract thought. It has become our experience that the present forms of thought will neither unlock the riddle of life nor reveal the secrets of our inner self with its other kind of experiences. A veil of woven pictures covers the depths of our own experience whenever our day-consciousness wanes at the edge of sleep. It is a veil of woven pictures also that the life of surrounding Nature becomes to us when with questioning soul we flow out into its expanses each time it begins to well forth in the spring, and when our perception draws back within us each time autumn brings about Nature's death and the darkness of winter deepens.

Does this breathing of our knowledge in a cosmic rhythm disclose anything more profound for our development? It does, and we can come into touch with it if we pay heed to our own cognitive processes; one does not take one's chair out into a landscape painting, or raise cabbages in the picture of a garden plot. The painting is at a distance from the viewer and communicates much of the personality of the artist who painted it. And while the character of the other person (the artist, in this case) takes on more distinct contours for us, we gain at the same time greater clarity about our own personality, abilities and strivings. . . . Basically we shape our own self-knowledge every time we extend our knowledge of another person. In the context of these reflections this means: Even though it behoves us in daily life to put our whole effort into what we do in the world, something altogether different can emerge in the course of our experiencing the world. Once we begin to see it as a picture, a twofold process is set going in us. The cognizing human spirit grows active and slowly finds its way through the pictures to their causative source. In this cognitive process of understanding the world, however, there takes place a further one that belongs to it as the mould to the cast: it is the cognitive process itself, that grasps hold of our own ego in reaching out to understand the world.

Thus the understanding of the world as a picture leads to man's own being. In reading the writing woven into Nature's veil by the spirituality active within her, we learn to decipher the riddle of man. We get to know ourselves. The urge to self-knowledge rising out of the depths of human nature turns our questioning eyes ceaselessly towards the world in an ever-renewed survey of Nature. And now that our inner being becomes an ever more burning question for us, now that time-worn answers no longer satisfy the urge for knowledge, the prevalent way of looking at Nature no longer satisfies either. Man is now seeking a new relationship to her because out of his prenatal existence he has brought with him an inkling of his own higher self, and this inkling prompts him to break through the official boundaries of knowledge. Man today, as he strives for and gains spiritual knowledge, no longer fits into the old conception of man established in the eighteenth and nineteenth centuries. The butterfly is slipping its cocoon and is about to leave the darkness it has been sleeping in and fly out into the light.

Thinking in Pictures—
A Social Force in our Time

The changing times in which we live are distinguished by a transformation that is taking place at a very deeply inward level in the
soul and spirit of modern humanity. The souls now approaching incarnation are bringing with them new forces and new impulses, but
these encounter a civilisation which has ossified in its old ideas and
its dependence on destructive abstract forces; in consequence what is
brought down as new forces and new aspirations in the will is far too
often barred from entry. Because of this Rudolf Steiner again and
again and with all emphasis drew attention, especially in younger
people, to what was so radically changing in humanity. In speaking
to a youthful audience such as gathered around him at Arnhem in
Holland in July 1924,[2] it was almost as if he wanted to hammer these
things right home into his listeners' souls, or rather, shall we say, to
hammer them from out of them; for they live there at the bottom of
every youthful soul today, but are sleeping.

He used most powerful words to wake them up: 'Ever since the
turn of the century the young people have had deep in their subconscious a particular kind of inner experience, whereby they feel
that something in the depths is rocking human development like an
earthquake.' 'From the very beginning it has seemed quite clear to
me that in their subconscious depths many of the younger generation today have a remarkably thorough understanding of the fact that
a great upheaval like an earthquake is going on which must change
the whole development of mankind. . . .' And again: 'The world
must be established anew from the very foundations up.' When we
hear these words we must ask ourselves: Where are the signs of this
tremendous transformation? Where can we come at the forces of
change that seek to bring in something utterly new, though as yet
but dimly felt by human beings? First and foremost we must mark
the ability to *think in pictures* which is beginning to have a most significant effect on the life of the modern soul. The picture is much

13

closer to man's supersensible experience than pictureless—in the literal sense unimaginative—abstract thinking. It is the first step towards loosening the bonds that hold us to the physical external world. When we develop a sense for the pictorial and arouse our fantasy into forming pictures, we are using the same force as works in the experience of actual spiritual reality in picture form, an experience attained with the first stage of supersensible knowledge, the stage of imaginative consciousness. It is based on man's formative forces. Accordingly, when we think in pictures we approach the very next stage of cognition lying above the normal thinking that is bound to the physical brain.

Let us consider the importance of this power of pictorial thinking for the general cultural development of man. In our anthroposophical studies, no matter how conscientious and thorough, many of us have certainly had to ask ourselves how far we have been simply meeting a purely subjective, egoistic need of our own, looking for some comfort of soul in these turbulent, discouraging times, and how far we have been striving towards the cultivation of forces which have actually to do in a positive sense with the distresses of the age. Are we really getting ourselves ready to bring help and healing into the surge of events, no matter in how humble a way? There is obviously no point in bending every problem we come across into an artificial connection with the general situation; it is rather a question of paying more careful attention to what is at work at a deeper level in the prevailing chaos as forces of soul and spirit. Rudolf Steiner can help us here, for he often spoke just in this sense about matters of the greatest importance.

He showed that the ability to think in pictures is something in the souls of the younger generation that has only recently begun to come into activity. Whereas from the beginning of the fifteenth to the end of the nineteenth century the soul forces that worked in man from out of the time before birth were quite pictureless, the souls of men since then have actually begun to bring *pictures* with them from the spiritual world. But: 'Pictures, if brought down from the spiritual into this physical life, must in all circumstances—if there is to be any salvation for mankind and for the social life—they must in all circumstances unite with the astral body, whereas pictureless ideas only enter the ego. After the middle of the fifteenth century humanity was largely occupied with bringing the ego to flower. But now the time has come when you must feel: Pre-natal pictures are living in you, and you must bring them alive during life. This you cannot do with the mere ego: it must go deeper down.'[3] That means, however, down to that region of the soul which is capable of experiencing feeling.

It is part of modern man's nature to resist letting the pictures experienced before conception radiate into the astral body. The sober and prosaic quality of our unimaginative era prevents a deeper response to what now seeks to enter the astral body. After all, there is a whole current of opinion today against even giving children such productions of creative imagination as fairy tales and legends. Anyone seeking to bring up children in true line with the needs of our time however must go quite the other way and make every effort *not* to kill these pre-natal pictures. If the teacher speaks out of the picture-creating power of his own soul, if for instance he presents the child with letters that are not just dead forms but developed out of pictures, if all the early teaching is actively borne along on this imaginative power of the soul, then the pre-natal powers of pictorial presentation are reinvigorated and enlivened.

But if they are deadened by a 'weary, stale, flat and unprofitable' education, by a lack of pictures, the child's astral body will develop destructive tensions: for the imaginative power will nonetheless unfold in the subsoil of the soul but, unable to rise into consciousness, will have a devastating, revolutionising effect. Such children grow up into unsatisfied adults who do not really know what they want. Indeed, they cannot know it, for as children they were given no help towards vivifying the pictures present in their souls. And so they rise up in opposition out of quite unconscious motives against the existing social forms, whose rigidity in turn prevents the new impulses they are bringing from the spiritual world from giving any new turn to the civilisation around them. With pictures from their life before birth, with heaven itself within their souls, they become destroyers of the present human order.

Thus we learn to understand that a force that is noble in itself yet working destructively in society is nothing other than the hidden impulse of new spiritual powers which are due to enter the social sphere. Many young people today unite in the conviction that the only way to a new order of things lies through the demolition of the old. As we listen to their outpourings we realise with well-nigh bleeding hearts that pure spiritual forces from the pre-natal existence may eventually be put to a work of sheer destruction. And why is this? It is because the spiritual re-shaping of civilisation is not keeping pace with the sublime spiritual impulses active in the souls now incarnating. What can we do to help these souls to unfold the heaven-born forces within them?

It may be surprising at first that Rudolf Steiner emphasises the soul rather than the spirit in the quotations above. Given the organisation of man into body, soul and spirit, one is accustomed to assign the spirit a place well above the 'mere' soul, which some spirit-seekers—such do actually exist!—consider as a thing 'to be overcome'. Rudolf Steiner gives a quite different assessment, according to which a man ought to employ all three members of his being in a harmonious manner. His spirit, particularly represented by the ego, has the power to grasp the purely spiritual and assimilate it without the use of pictures. At a level of human development where this ego cannot yet properly manage the capacities for higher knowledge involved, say, at the stage of knowledge defined by Rudolf Steiner in an exact sense as intuition, there is always the risk of one-sidedness in its way of looking at the world, of its not using all its forces in due measure but allowing the soul, and consequently the feeling, too little share in the cognitive process. But the soul is the link between the spirit and the body: it carries the spiritual impulses, invigorating them with feeling, down into the earthly realm.

The course of human development made it necessary for the ego first of all to settle down on earth solely with its pure spiritual powers. This came about gradually in that it first worked in the astral body, developing the sentient soul during the Egyptian–Chaldean cultural epoch; in the Greco–Latin period it was active in the ether-body, fashioning the rational soul; and since the fifteenth century it has been taking hold of the physical body itself and therefore making particular use of the physical brain as an organ of knowledge. The soul, which is chiefly at home in the sentient body, has been keeping more in the background. Now, however, it is important to understand in this connection that one of the changes taking place at the present time in humanity is coming about because our souls are now bringing with them a greater abundance of pre-natal spirituality, particularly in the form of pictures.

Pictures as such are actually a means whereby the etheric in man finds expression. Even unconscious sense-impressions and purely conceptual cognitions stamp themselves as pictures into the ether body. But pictures thus unconsciously imprinted do not come into our consciousness until after we have passed through the gates of death. If they are already to become effective as formative forces in earthly life itself and have an active bearing on the outside world, they must be taken up by the astral body, which is the member of man's being that feels and comprehends, and is indeed the creator of consciousness as such. For only in this way do they become inward in man, a part of his personal individuality.

It mattered enormously to Rudolf Steiner that anthroposophical knowledge should not remain merely in the ego but that it should be *taken inside* and encompass the soul, the middle sphere of man at its deepest. Therefore he once described what he regarded as the real beginning of the anthroposophical movement in the following way:* 'Anthroposophy does not come alive as long as there are none but those who bring only their sometimes extreme cleverness to bear on it and profess it simply as a set of ideas. The moment, however, that souls feel like bursting with rapture and are thrilled with joy at one or another aspect of some especially important truth, only then and not before, in such people as feel themselves to be anthroposophists, is the anthroposophical movement born. It is born, it really begins to exist as anthroposophical movement only in the whole man. Then it also comes of itself into a state of equilibrium.—Now, my dear friends, I would like to send you away from this lecture with this question very much in mind: How far here and now are we capable of catching fire within and rejoicing in sheer rapture at anthroposophical ideas?—Then from this point of view just think about the beginning of the anthroposophical movement.'

The unceasing effort to promote these interiorising forces of the soul pervades Rudolf Steiner's whole attitude, his every word and deed like a leitmotif. This enables us to understand, for instance, why he sought in every way to help us acquire an inner artistic attitude in every sphere of life. In this he did not mean that everybody ought to take on some kind of art as a profession, but that something of the true inner freedom of the artist which is born of spiritual experience should come to life in us, even to the extent of influencing our way of regarding and judging other people. Time and again he therefore admonished the Waldorf School teachers not to judge a child's mistakes in an abstractly moralising way but to go into its peculiarities intimately and to experience them artistically in the above sense: for this attitude gives birth to the creative helping deed, to an actual healing force, and not to mere reproof or condemnation. This also explains the value attributed to pictures and images in Rudolf Steiner education for a child's development, as has already been indicated. So let us now ask: If these picture-creating forces in a child's soul are not put an end to by unimaginative teaching but are called into play by presenting knowledge in the form of living pictures, how does the child or adolescent become conscious of them? How do they evolve? This question could be answered in detail only if we could see exactly how such a child fares subsequently in its whole development of soul. Failing this, and apart from the fact that it is not in a child's nature to speak of its experiences in this connection, we can nevertheless learn something from what we already know ourselves of actual children who have been educated on Steiner's lines.

The child becomes altogether more inwardly alive, more directly itself in what it says and does, because its inner forces of imagination are not being killed off. It is able to do more out of itself in artistic work, and it may then well be that a great deal in its painting and modelling will reflect the pictures living on in its own depths, fashioned by the soul-forces formative in these and pulsating upwards into outer deed. An inner creative power thus preserved and stimulated leads in later life to a more intimate feeling and understanding for another's experience, to an insight into his being from within. And this is after all the ground out of which in reality that inner activity can grow, which in his *Philosophy of Freedom*[4] Rudolf Steiner calls moral imagination, and which eventually gives birth to new social forces in the soul. And finally, such an encouragement of inner powers in childhood, which are eventually understood and wielded consciously, can lead on to a path of spiritual striving entirely free of mere abstraction. Taken to their consequent conclusion, such thoughts as these bring home to us the possibilities open to these formative picture-forces for fundamentally changing the inner life of mankind, if only they are properly cultivated. We can also see how Waldorf education, in striving to advance the development of humanity along these lines, is important not at all solely for the few, relatively speaking, who have the opportunity to work in it, but for the evolution of social forces in general: Waldorf education is pre-eminently a social factor carrying anthroposophy into the cultural life of the world.

When Steiner for the first time gave a whole cycle of lectures specifically for younger people—it was the *Pedagogical Youth Course*[5] given in the autumn of 1922, and his listeners had come together around him as their spiritual leader—he could, as he said himself, speak in quite a different way from the usual. Years of study of the Youth Course can lead to a deep experience of this difference in the style of expression of which he is speaking. One particular feature is the distinctively pictorial form of presentation. Not that these pictures come into the foreground: they are woven into the entirety of the Youth Course as an imaginative element of language. But after each of these pictures has been examined by itself, all of them taken together give a series that takes the viewer back from his present-day experiences through manifold transformations of varying effect to a single great and sublime imagination, which those who have incarnated since the end of the nineteenth century all beheld before birth: the imagination of Michael fighting and vanquishing the dragon. Rudolf Steiner laid down this pathway through the pictures in the Youth Course as an inner path of transformation and development that can lead to a direct knowledge of the life before birth. On this occasion therefore, when he wanted to arouse certain impulses which were now fast asleep in the young people around him, he himself made a very special use, alive and fruitful, of the picture-forces. And as a spiritual researcher he shows in his own practice the perfect handling of these deepening, inwardising powers. He tells us how there had also been spiritual researchers before him, but they not only backed away from the abstract scientific knowledge that was fast coming in at the time, but also never got beyond a dreamlike knowledge of the Moon-sphere, whereas it was his task to penetrate up into the Saturn-sphere and so to enable himself to describe the cosmic evolution from its beginning, on Ancient Saturn, as he subsequently did in his *Occult Science*.[6] To write this book 'I made the attempt to take into my inner experience the completely conscious world of ideas that otherwise relates only to outer objects of nature and to impregnate the imaginative world with it. This then made it possible for me to penetrate into the whole sequence of Saturn, Sun and Moon.' The difference between modern science and what he has given through this procedure is that 'the modern scientist can only call on his ego in his investigations, and begins to dream as soon as ever he comes out of it, whereas I could also tell the astral body the ideas the scientists work with, and so enable it to penetrate into the worlds I had to describe'.*

What Rudolf Steiner says here about his own methods of research can throw further light on what was quoted above. While the earlier spiritual researchers worked in a more dreamlike way, shrinking back from investigating the physical world, he himself, by making his way down into the depths of the materialistic view of Nature, was able in his researches to rise all the higher into the world of spirit.

Thus we stand before *one* of the great transformations in the souls of present-day humanity. If we wish to understand the newer powers at work in them, it is no use turning to general conceptions about the constitution, consciousness and development of the human being, for these apply equally to the humanity of earlier centuries. There are of course laws of evolution that are valid for long ages, even if not for ever. But there are also peculiarities only belonging to human beings of a particular epoch, and these must not be ignored if we are to obtain a valid picture of the period concerned. And one of the peculiarities of the present day is that human souls are turning to the picture.

The Second Man in Us

In considering the origin of thinking in pictures and the need to foster it in children, we have so far been concerned with the age around the change of teeth. Pictorial thinking, however, also needs such fostering beyond this age, so let us now turn to the change occurring at the end of the next seven-year period.

It was in the lectures about karma and its laws which Rudolf Steiner gave on the occasion of the Agricultural Course at Breslau, that he came to talk about this subject. It is necessary, he said, to educate oneself into a quite special devotion towards life, for without devotion life will not come into that deepening it absolutely needs if civilization is to make any progress at all. 'The whole life of soul must grow more intimate, more inwardly fine and delicate; then we shall see something of the real nature of this life again. Then we shall look out from within human development itself at the pre-terrestrial life.'[7] And then also we shall understand more intimately the metamorphosis that comes about in the adolescent when he reaches the so-called awkward age. His awkwardness is only too plain for everyone to see, but the subtle processes going on within his soul can only be understood by those who acquire something of the inner perceptiveness Rudolf Steiner is speaking about. For after sexual maturity a second man gradually makes his appearance in this youthful being, 'a second, cloud-like man within the man. And we need this perception of that second, cloud-like man in man. Everywhere today there arise questions relating to this second man. But our civilisation does not answer them.' And once again Rudolf Steiner points out that an extraordinary change took place in the spiritual development of the earth at the turn of the nineteenth and twentieth centuries, and that the Light-Age, long awaited and foretold by eastern man, then made its beginning. With this there is connected the fact that in the youthful heart and mind there now lives the yearning to know more about the real nature of man, to learn to look at man more closely. But our

21

present civilization just has no answer to offer to its questions. The whole Youth Movement* was born out of this yearning for a deeper understanding of man. It was this second, cloud-like man, who comes forth after sexual maturity, that those taking part in the Youth Movement wanted to understand. What is this second man? 'It is that one who lived in the previous incarnation, and who now enters shadow-like into the present life.' And therefore out of their new spiritual forces younger people are really asking about destiny, about the way to recognise their own destinies.

Let us take a historical look at this transformation in man's seeking. In the eighteenth and nineteenth centuries German culture shows us many human souls turning to superphysical experiences. Notably it was the romantics who tried to grasp these 'night-sides of human nature'. What loving care did Justinus Kerner bestow on his Seeress of Prevorst! How magnificently did Goethe describe in his novel *Wilhelm Meister* the increasing power of knowledge in a Makarie! These souls came to be at home in the preternatural, but usually they did so in a peculiar way: namely, through a body-free expansion into extra-human and extra-terrestrial realms, mostly with the surrender, however, of their self-consciousness, through a going-out-of-themselves into *space*. And only very special individuals pierced, also in their own way, the boundaries of *time*, and so came to an understanding of repeated earthly lives, as did, for example, Lessing, Goethe and Novalis.

The fact that this second, cloud-like man is working so strongly and thus giving rise to so many questions in the souls today, again points to one of those inner metamorphoses which the present age is bringing about: it is the development of a more intense consciousness of the soul and spirit of man, a development that begins in puberty. Of course a small child also has active in it its astral-, its star-body, the vehicle of its feelings and of musical experience, but with the child this astral body is around it, it envelops it, interlacing and weaving itself through it from the outside. This astral body of a small child contains shining forms of light as a kind of imprint of all the experiences of the soul's pre-natal, cosmic existence. During the years of childhood these forms of light gradually fade and are drawn inside the organism, so that about the time of puberty the process is complete; then these forms of light wholly merge with the organs of the human body. It is not until this moment that the astral body becomes an individual part of the young person, linking him to the cosmic forces by means of these organs; in this way the cloud-like man is literally drawn into the human being. And even though the ego does not attain independence until the 21st year, it does already begin to exert a greater influence at this earlier time by way of the astral body. Now this astral-ego member, which unites more closely with the physical-etheric at puberty, comes into consciousness today much more intensely than in times past; that is the significant change. The fact that this astral-ego nature becomes more conscious drives up many questions into the soul, just those questions about one's own eternal man who is the bearer of karmic development.

When we observe young people at this age, it is easy enough to see that on the one hand a much more strongly coloured and often vehement emotional life has set in. Antipathies, in particular, now come out in many ways more intensely and as often as not, it would seem, without any reason. The real cause actually lies in the karmic relationships to other individual people, which now begin to sound out much more loudly into life. On the other hand we can see a really hungering interest in the great interconnections of history, in all that throws light on the development of man, which is after all nothing but that path of the ego of mankind with which each individual destiny is united by so many bonds. It is as if the young human being were groping his way through a veil of sympathy and antipathy towards a more intensive understanding of one or other part of human history which up till then had remained unfamiliar in its earthly aspect to his own inner being. The age-old γνῶθι σαυτόν (gnothi sautón, know thy self), the 'Who am I?' is sounding in his soul. 'If a completely honest member of today's Youth Movement were to wake up one morning in such a way as to have all the night's experiences standing vividly before him for a quarter of an hour, and if he were to be asked during that time: What is it you are really striving for?— then he would say: I want to come to an understanding of the whole man, the one, that is, who has gone through repeated earthly lives. I want to know what is living in my own inner self from earlier stages of existence. You, however, know nothing at all about it. You don't tell me anything about it.—In human souls today there is the urge to understand and get to the bottom of karma.'[7] That was Rudolf Steiner's way of describing this problem in Breslau. It is the sovereign ancestor of one's own being that asks to be understood. It is readily understandable why those souls with supersensible experience in the eighteenth and nineteenth centuries were less able to perceive repeated incarnations and quite unable to follow the laws of karma, for the state of human consciousness was different then: the ego had not yet come into the foreground of experience to the same extent as now. And it is after all the ego that as the spiritual nucleus in each human being passes through repeated earth-lives.

This question about destiny, about the fact of reincarnation comes up in the soul with such intensity these days that younger people have hardly any difficulty in accepting what anthroposophy has to say about it. We are here faced with one of those soul-transformations that occurred in the younger generation about the turn of the century. In his *Youth Course*[5] and in his various addresses to younger people[2] Rudolf Steiner threw a revealing light on this metamorphosis, for he was well acquainted with something we can often experience with the young nowadays: they not only carry the inner question within them, they have not only brought the certainty of reincarnation down into earthly life, but more frequently than some might believe they have quite distinct inner experiences of actual facts out of previous incarnations. Failure to understand these things accurately in relation to the great general connections behind them can lead to serious inner confusion. It is a matter of facing oneself and one's inner experience clearly and soberly, and of intensive work at an understanding of man as spiritual science describes him. But it is also important to cultivate and develop a very special power of the soul, which alone makes possible a knowledge of karmic connections and facts of previous incarnations, and which Rudolf Steiner so greatly emphasises: it is the power of selfless love.

Selfless love must become an organ of knowledge. Rudolf Steiner lays special stress on it in this connection: selfless love even for oneself! It is almost easier to attain the purification of feeling implied in regard to another being than to one's own existence; for in regard to this vanity, desire of recognition and suchlike things easily make their way in. These dangers, however, must be risked; it will not do to suppress or reject through fear what has been working in all souls born since the end of the nineteenth century to give them the special stamp and task the present incarnation in its general human quality requires. For that would mean to retard evolution.

This 'second, cloud-like man' is not at all to be taken as just a picturesque expression. He is an active reality that begins to work in that transformation of the human sheath-relationships which takes place at puberty. Rudolf Steiner raised him into our consciousness for the reason that only that part of the self we are actually conscious of can be gradually turned, so to say, into a tool, into a chisel where-with the ego can shape itself and thus give a definite direction to all it contributes to the development of mankind.

The process of the metamorphosis of human consciousness can be pictured in something like the following phases. The general evolu-tion of mankind gives rise to certain changes in the souls of people living at any particular time. These changes are at first recognised only by a few individuals, either as a matter of their own experience or of observing them in others. Expressed by artists or explained and applied by scientists (unfortunately not always in the right way) such phenomena are thus brought to the consciousness of the many others who of themselves were not waking up to them with the same inner attention. Only when this new range of experience has thus been opened up to the general consciousness can it be quarried for what is needed for the new edifices of civilization, which in their principal lines are always and only determined by some very few leading spirits, whether for better or for worse.

It will now be clear how important it is for such a growing aware-ness of a new experience not to get bogged down in mere sensational-ism, as has happened with some recent writers. Neither must this consciousness be taken up by traditional types of thinking and forced into mental grooves that can never lead towards a healthy future de-velopment. Accordingly it is all the more important that for the artist and scientist discovering this new field of experience Rudolf Steiner in his spiritual research has provided a sure basis of knowledge; it offers a path into the future which is entirely right and suitable for our times. Moreover, as regards the individual as such, it is also on this basis alone that a self-knowledge and a conscious self-develop-ment towards the true future of man can be achieved.

Where a new forming of the inner life is being attempted out of anthroposophy, it is in this sense of fundamental importance to raise the second man in us ever more clearly into consciousness. For the second man, as described here, can be understood by anyone at all who is able to open himself to the knowledge of man such as the new ideas and lines of thought of spiritual science provide. Furthermore, this knowledge of the second man serves as the cognitive basis for anyone aiming at his own inner self-forming along the new paths shown to us by Rudolf Steiner.

We know that it belongs to this way of development to form a living connection between willing and thinking. To carry forces of life and will into thinking, and clarity of thought into willing is demanded of us along this path. But this in no way means that earthly thinking and earthly willing should be coupled together to the exclusion of the middle forces of feeling! On the contrary, through concerning ourselves with the second, cloud-like man and his entry into the human being at puberty, we come to see with precision the deeper aspects of this modern inner way. One-sided exercise of a will not yet cleansed of egoism will not take one along this path; neither will breathing exercises, such as had their complete justification only in much earlier times. Here it is rather a matter of consciously grasping what now in this century demands to be thus grasped as never before, as it rises up—as never before—out of the depths of the soul and waits to be given its shape. And that is the second man in us.

Anyone who attains a genuine experience of this inner man by strengthening his inner attentiveness in the way indicated by Rudolf Steiner in *Knowledge of the Higher Worlds*[1] and other writings, will realize as a fact, altogether surprising at first, that he experiences this spirit-form as a man placed upside down above or inside him. But it is the same with everything. It is the same with the plants, which grow from below upwards, while their spiritual equivalent grows from above downwards.* It is the same with the crystal forms, whose spiritual equivalents provided the paths along which the forces streamed in that shaped the physical crystal in the first place; in the case of quartz for example, this spiritual form is a counter-pyramid, a supersensible counter-form, which rises up, upside down, on the crystal's apex—it is relatively easy to perceive for anyone who occupies himself with crystals in the right way. Such a spiritual counter-form exists also for human beings, and that is the second, cloud-like man in us. He thrusts down into the physical body—to use one of Rudolf Steiner's similes—like a sword into its sheath.

Now the soul-spirit aspect of this physical body does not look like that which we see when we are awake. If someone approaches the threshold to the spiritual world, he sees the forces as such that form this physical body and not the earthly matter it consists of. He then experiences how in the lower part of the body those hierarchical powers hold sway that are seen in the picture of the Bull, in the middle part in the picture of the Lion, and in the head in that of the Eagle— the whole united by the ego-countenance of the Man: they are the four principal animals of the zodiac, which are experienced by Grossmann in Albert Steffen's drama *Das Viergetier*.[8] This spiritual picture can be grasped as a whole or in part at waking, when the higher members of our being look down on the sleeping body at rest, in which these exalted hierarchic beings are ruling. The same sight opens out to us, however, when we look in the right way at our own body at the Threshold. How far this fourfold imprinting seal of man is distorted or harmonious in its shape shows us the amount of damage our own actions have caused to it as spirit-form.

But the second man sinks down into the physical body in such a way that his head is united with the region of the lower physical man, where the Bull reigns, and the Eagle of the second man is transformed into the Scorpion. The middle of the cloud-like man, where the Lion is active, joins the Lion powers of our physical body, so that the middle forces of the physical and etheric and of the soul and spirit are woven together. Where the Eagle-forces work out of cosmic heights into the physical head, there the Bull radiates in from the spiritual man—the Bull, whose forces we feel particularly in our speaking. We now have this arrangement:

Physical man	*The second man in us*
Eagle	Bull
Lion	Lion
Bull	Eagle

Now when the human being consciously embarks on a path of inner schooling, he must activate and strengthen the cloud-like second man, and indeed raise him so intensively into consciousness that his powers are not dulled by those of the physical man. Then the second man's sphere of knowledge will begin to be effective in the physical man's sphere of will: thinking will be carried into willing. Conversely, the higher man's will powers can come to irradiate the upper physical man's thinking: our thoughts will then acquire the mobility of spiritual limbs and spiritual organs of touch, so that when we strengthen the second man in us we can grasp spirituality in knowledge by touching it.

If we take in the full meaning of this, we will understand the enormous responsibility associated with the present point of time: the second man, previously cultivated only in secluded schools of occult training, is now gradually beginning to enter the experience of mankind as a whole. It is time to lay hold of him in full consciousness. If we set out on the path of spiritual training with all exactitude in inner activity, we come to moments of pure concentration when we raise the second man out of the physical body and with him and through him win a new understanding of man and of the world. And this we do, not by surrendering our ego-consciousness, but precisely as egos. For the second, cloud-like man is closely connected with our star-like astral body, the bearer and sheath of our ego.

This is a second, deeper aspect opened up to us by our considerations of the cloud-like man within us.

We must be aware, however, that all the powers of hindrance are united at the present time to prevent our learning how to understand and handle the second man in us. The catastrophes of our modern social and political life are powerfully deflecting many a path of development. This gives rise to forces entirely hostile to genuine human progress. The great emphasis on the intellect demanded by present-day science kills man's spiritual powers and from earliest school days on so cramps and hardens what should be kept alive and in movement that as often as not a cure hardly comes in question for the rest of life. To crown it all, philosophies and *Weltanschauungen* are now coming up which batter entirely false ideas into the heads of people with the aim of keeping out of them such knowledge of spirit as is in anthroposophy.

It is a time of strife we are living in, because the direction to be taken by the whole stream of evolution in the future is at stake. We must be quite conscious of this. Only so can there be given to each of our thoughts and words, to each of our deeds that degree of responsibility which alone justifies our occupation with these problems of spiritual science.

The New Pictorial Perception and its Meaning for Mankind Today

The previous chapters have shown that we cannot meet the demands of our time unless we become aware of the great transformation that took place in the pre-natal sphere at the turn of the last century: the transformation from abstract thinking connected chiefly with the ego, to pictorial thinking. Let us now consider more exactly the essential difference between the two.

The ego is man's spiritual nucleus; it needs a soul to link it to the physical world in which it is to unfold its activity. It also needs and builds the physical body to be, as we might say, its physiognomical expression in each of its earthly lives. Hence there is a special connection between the ego and its physical body. Now we can visualize how this spiritual kernel of man brings impulses with it out of the exalted regions it traverses between death and rebirth, which not only concern its own impending earthly life but also what is to take place in the epoch as a whole. In preparation therefore for our present period, that of the consciousness-soul, not only were these ego-impulses very much intensified, but at the same time the ego itself had to strike right down into the physical world: for the task of the consciousness-soul is gradually to come to a full recognition of the spirit in the physical world. Now for the achievement of this certain preparatory stages were necessary, and in one of these it was essential for the ego to immerse itself completely in the material world, which the human spirit had in no way ever taken hold of so intensely before, or indeed learnt to control to any extent at all. If the human ego is completely immersed in the physical, however, there develop in consequence the twin capacities of wide-awake, purely physical sense-perception and intellectual thinking, the capacities, that is, which originated in the fifteenth century and were systematically perfected in eighteenth- and nineteenth-century materialism.

While this was developing, the soul life of man, mediating as we have said between the material world and the spirit, underwent a special schooling in the experience of matter. The fact that just in the soul itself we have an organ with which we can also experience the spiritual that is at work in the physical world was pushed into the background, and in our own day it has disappeared so far below the horizon of general consciousness that the possibility of such soul-experience is generally denied.

The central impulse in the souls incarnating from the fifteenth to the nineteenth century was to unfold the life of the ego, but to do so as a denizen of the physical world and thus as particularly dependent on the ego's activity in the physical body and its organs. Therefore it resulted in intellectual thought rather than in pictorial consciousness, for pictorial consciousness does not encompass the physical-mineral world.

With the coming of the nineteenth century, a mighty preparation took place in the spiritual world for the impending world-transformation. The souls about to incarnate about the turn of the century passed through an exalted school of training there and were instructed in the Sun-Mystery of Christ in 'wondrous, majestic imaginations'.* What they had themselves experienced in the mystery-centres of old now had to rise up out of their soul-depths, but in a way that wakened new impulses for the future. We can surmise what forces and what aims for spiritual development such visions must have instilled into the souls for their next life on earth. After the age of materialism, how could the world-transformation signified by the dawn of the Light-Age have been launched in any other way? Those human beings now ready for incarnation were to be helpers in the inauguration of this epoch into the world of men; humanity's entire line of vision had to be readjusted. 'The spiritual world has assumed another attitude to the physical world'; that is how Rudolf Steiner characterized this change. And the souls are in fact gradually transforming their activity in so far as they are now having to recognise what is beyond the merely physical. But there is more to the establishment of a new form of consciousness on earth than this: it involves many fundamental changes right down into the forms of human social life.

Such an immense change in the coming epoch of mankind called for a corresponding preparation in the spiritual world. It necessitated a new capacity in human souls for physical existence. The seeds were implanted for evolving a different attitude to the earthly world from the one previously described, a new use of consciousness that would lead the souls back to spiritual perception. It follows that the exalted pre-natal experiences we have spoken of did not involve only the spirit in man, they were not only grasped by the ego, but they were imprinted as picture straight into the newly-forming ether-body, so that they would exert their power from out of the inner life-substance of the physical body in the next earthly life.

Mighty indeed were these proceedings in the spiritual world, as we can judge from Rudolf Steiner's disclosure that at the time the super-sensible 'Cultus', as he called it, was taking place certain special souls even on earth were irradiated by it. Goethe and Schiller, for example, both of them leading spirits of the German people, caught sight in miniature, as it were, of what was happening and embodied it in words. Thus we find Schiller, who in his spirit cherished such high ideals for the development of man, writing the *Letters on the Aesthetic Education of Man*, in which he sought the true, state-building forces that might offer the free man a basis for his development. He was the first German to formulate in these Letters the threefold membering of the human being: starting out from the opposed compulsions in human nature that are exerted by the body and the reason, he thought his way through to what arises in the 'middle man' between them as the impulse towards the beautiful and the truly free.

And we can see a vision awakening in the depths of Goethe's soul which enabled him to fetch down a 'miniature picture', as Rudolf Steiner calls it, of those mighty spiritual events in his *Fairy Tale of the Green Snake and the Beautiful Lily.** It is a deeply moving thought which has something of a blessing in it that at a time when such awe-inspiring events were taking place in the spiritual world, human souls were able by dint of pure and persevering struggle to receive them into their souls, even if only in images.

Yet another great event took place in the spiritual world as the nineteenth century progressed. Rudolf Steiner told how the retarding Ahrimanic spirits, who opposed the work of Michael, were conquered in a mighty battle and thrust down into the earthly world, so that in the spiritual world itself the road was clear for Michael's leadership. This battle and this victory of Michael's were likewise witnessed by the souls awaiting incarnation, and they have been bringing the impression down to earth with them since the turn of the century as an impelling picture that works deep below within their life of soul. It was to this picture that Rudolf Steiner led the souls in the autumn of 1922, when he closed the lectures of the *Youth Course* with the description of this battle.

We have asked the question: What does pictorial consciousness mean? Now we have seen that when these two tremendous, all-significant events took place in the spiritual world, they left the deepest possible impression on the souls that witnessed them. Just in these two events therefore we can recognize what was happening in this soul-metamorphosis and whither it was tending.

Now whereas from the fifteenth to the nineteenth century the ego-impulse veered strongly towards physical experience, the pictures impressed into the ether-body before birth, such as those just described, must also come into consciousness during life on earth if during that life they are themselves to remain alive. 'Pictures, if brought down into the physical life, must in all circumstances—if there is to be any salvation for mankind and the social life—they must in all circumstances unite with the astral body'.[3] For the astral body is the vehicle of consciousness: without it we would in fact be unconscious. It is the astral body, the soul, and not the physical body which these pictures must join forces with.

How can this be done? How can a man bring these pictures into union with his astral body?

The chapter on thinking in pictures discussed the general methods of education that can bring this about. Let us now examine pictorial vision itself and its expression in the processes and activities of the various members of the human organization. Then we shall be able to see how to come to it through conscious development.

How then does any kind of pictorial experience come about?

A certain kind of picture consciousness is familiar to all of us, namely the dream. During sleep the astral body and the ego are drawn to a considerable extent out of the physical and etheric bodies. When we fall asleep or awaken, we have a moment when the connection is loose enough—but not too loose—for the astral body to look as it were at the ether-body it is in the process of leaving or returning to. We thus obtain a brief consciousness of our ether-body, and the ether-body's means of bringing itself to our notice is the *picture*. Whenever we have any consciousness of our ether-body, or of anything spiritual the perception of which involves the ether-body, we see pictures. It is so at the moment of death, when the whole ether-body leaves the physical body, and it is the same at a certain phase of spiritual training, when we come to look at our ether-body consciously: in both cases the panorama of life is spread before us. Pictures likewise arise if the separated astral body perceives something of its processes inside the ether-body, when this has not entirely parted company with the physical body, as in sleep or again in states of higher consciousness.

Anything not of a physical-mineral nature is perceived by pictorial vision and not with the physical senses. The ether-body is not physical: although it weaves throughout our earthly body, infusing it with life, its substance is of cosmic origin. A non-physical object, e.g. the ether-body of a plant, cannot be perceived by our physical senses but by that which is super-physical in us, the ether-body, and the ether-body's perception consists in the production of pictures. But these pictures do not reach our consciousness unless they are received by the astral or soul-body.

Picture consciousness is therefore brought about by a special activity of the soul-body.

Now this soul-body has been educated for centuries only to concern itself, while awake, with physical objects. In other words, it has been all this time simply a servant of the ego's activity in physical existence, which has consisted entirely in assembling external information of little consequence to the soul in order to achieve control of the material world. This has led to an atrophy within the soul-body, so that there has been no development of that strong life of feeling through which alone the surging depths of experience come into action and give rise to a consciousness free of the physical body. That is why we can carry into our day-consciousness hardly anything of the sublime experiences our ego and astral body go through during sleep; all we can remember nowadays is more or less distorted dream-images. It was at this juncture in the soul-evolution of mankind that Rudolf Steiner intervened in an entirely practical way and showed how the path could be rightly trodden today towards a clear experience of the spiritual. Through all he gave he enabled us to take ourselves in hand and develop that member of our being, the astral body, which is chiefly responsible for our emotional life and therefore links together body and spirit, physical and spiritual world. If we follow the teaching he offered, we can gradually train the astral body to perceive not only the physical world, but also the spirituality which weaves everywhere throughout it.

If humanity, therefore, is to develop towards an exact perception of spiritual reality, it will have to educate and form its astral body in a special way.

The astral body, however, is that member of man's being that was seduced by the Luciferic temptation into going its own independent way to such an extent that it turned to the material world against the will of the higher divine worlds. This Luciferic temptation signifies a turning, a catastrophe in the development of mankind, in the literal meaning of the Greek term χαταστροφή, the turning-point in a drama. The divine leading powers have been working unceasingly ever since to heal the evil effects of this catastrophe. At the present time we are quite evidently standing at a special stage in this line of events, characterized as it is by the tremendous battle raging over the future path to be followed by mankind. It is indeed one of the features distinguishing our time from the past that this decision is now in the hands of man's own free will, free will that is based on knowledge.

If we look at the manifold strivings which have been undertaken in the course of human history in connection with this, we can recognize, amongst the teachings proffered to man, two which are particularly important, owing to their relationship in time to the path taken by the Christ-Being Himself. There is first of all Christ's own activity on earth, His physical life; then in connection with it, are the Gospels, the writings presenting to us the facts of this Christ-life, and necessary since the human soul is not yet so far on that it can approach the life of Christ on earth with its own power of inner perception. Christ is indeed the Being Who endowed earthly and human existence with the power enabling man gradually to work his way up again from his lowest level back to his own real origin, to the Spirit, whilst the Gospels are the sole documents telling us about the deeds of Christ on earth. Now among these it is the Gospel of St. John which is composed in such a way as to work towards the purification of the astral body—which is the problem we are concerned with here in the first place.

The other path that comes into consideration is the one along which we are striving forward towards spiritual communion with each other in the present age: it is anthroposophy. While the Gospels are a manual of schooling that seeks to impart what Christ showed forth in His life amongst His intimate disciples and all those who witnessed His life *on earth*, Rudolf Steiner's teachings were given to mankind as a path which is in special connection with the *cosmic* path of the Christ Being, in order to help it at a time when Christ Himself begins to be active among men in a new and special way: having formerly lived among *physical* men, He is now approaching human *souls* in the spiritual sphere closest to the physical, in an etheric form. Rudolf Steiner's aim was to help the souls to form themselves in such a way that they will not remain blind to this new activity of Christ; it is the special characteristic of the anthroposophical path.

The two paths merge at an important point, in that both of them lead, at a certain stage, to a pictorial experience of the life of Christ. Rudolf Steiner gave a special help in this regard in his cycles of lectures on the Gospels, through which these have become, as it were, an integral part of anthroposophical teaching.

The Shaping of the Inner Man

If a modern human being sets out on a path of inner training, of conscious self-development, he will have to activate his higher man, the second man in him, to bring about a change in his whole character. We have frequently mentioned this second man and seen that the sentient or astral body plays an important part in his development.

The astral body is the vehicle of the soul, but it is also active in our sense-perceptions: from it all our power of experience radiates outwards and inwards. Outer world and inner world, physical, bodily experience as well as that of the soul and spirit find in the astral body a common field of consciousness. During the most recent epoch of human development the main trend of our inner experience—the sequence of our thoughts, the shaping of our feelings, and the aims of our will—has been towards the comprehension and control of the outer world. In consequence our inner life has become immensely dependent, both as regards its direction and its ideas about itself, on a form of thinking which keeps as closely as possible in line with outer phenomena.

Anyone who embarks on a path of training must give the three functions of his soul-body—thinking, feeling and willing—a new direction, but he must do so in a balanced and harmonious way. When a special attempt is made today to train the will to be strong and purposeful—as often as not for purely utilitarian reasons—it leads to a pronounced onesidedness, since thinking and feeling will fail to keep pace with the will-training and continue to work in the old way.

This is why the soul's three powers of thinking, feeling and willing must be transformed in mutual harmony. Modern man will need to begin with thinking, because there he attains his highest degree of consciousness and is better able to survey and control what is taking place. In his thinking he is awake and so is in a position to be free.

Thus it was that Rudolf Steiner first approached the general public

with his book *The Philosophy of Freedom*,[4] which is concerned with
human thinking. In thinking, the ego is active, and above all in the
ether-body. From here it takes hold of the bodily organs of thought
as its physical basis, especially certain parts of the forebrain. If the
brain of a person whose thinking is still very dependent on it is
affected in some way, perhaps by injury, then his thinking will be
disturbed. This will not be so marked if the thinking has already
detached itself to a certain extent from its bodily foundation and has
become body-free. In *The Philosophy of Freedom* Rudolf Steiner has
given us a method of transforming our thinking to such a degree that
the transformation will also embrace the whole sentient body and
purify it.[9] All the same, it was no teaching of Rudolf Steiner's that
the only way to such purification is through a study of *The Philosophy
of Freedom*. On the contrary, he pointed out more than once that
there are various methods of bringing about catharsis. And when in
1924 he told me of his intention to revise a number of his books for
the benefit of young people, his reason was, '. . . after all I wrote a
book like *The Philosophy of Freedom* for people over the age of
28 . . .'* It would have been foreign to his whole nature to set up any
kind of dogmatic thesis. And he did in fact give various introductions
to the path of knowledge, as for example the series of exercises
in *Knowledge of the Higher Worlds*,[1] those in *Occult Science*,[6]
certain instructions in *A Road to Man's Self-knowledge*,[10] and others
as well.

Turning now from the soul-functions to the members of the human
being, we become aware that this sort of self-training first of all involves a loosening of the ether-body. In line with the post-Atlantean
task of grasping the material world, the ether-body has been drawn
more and more into the physical body. An ancient Atlantean's ether-
head extended considerably beyond the outlines of his physical head.
This enabled him to perceive the ether-world and influence it. In the
course of time the ties between the ether-body and the physical body
grew stronger: man obtained a sharper and better defined perception
of the world in its purely physical outlines, while his perception, experience and thought of anything not purely mineral diminished.

Now that mankind has the task of returning to pictorial experience,
these close connections between the ether-body and the physical body
must be loosened again. In practice, this is done by strengthening
one's ability to form ideas free of the senses and in an intensive way

to direct all one's attention to the superphysical. It is in high measure that the early exercises given in *Knowledge of the Higher Worlds* help towards achieving this. Such an activity loosens the ether-body out of its tight enmeshment with the physical organs so that it can expand and become increasingly mobile. This gives rise to a receptivity for non-physical processes such as those to be found within the world of growth. There also develops a much stronger capacity of a body-free order for experiencing, for a feeling together with everything of a soul-nature in the surroundings; this in turn leads to a knowledge regarding the inner life of others that calls for much tact and self-control if the freedom of others and therefore the harmony of a community are not to suffer. The problems which arise everywhere today in connection with human life together are in fact an indication that man is already beginning as a matter of course to loosen and expand his ether-body.

In the inner life this stage of development often announces itself in a typical picture that may occur in a dream or in moments of inner concentration. It is the so-called abyss-experience, in which the person concerned finds himself—often with great anxiety—as if standing at the brink of an abyss, or perhaps as if hovering over it. Sometimes reminiscences of an earlier mountaineering mishap will play in, though it can happen without these, and then he will be hanging helplessly on the face of a cliff over a terrifying chasm with no foot-hold whatsoever to support him. Eventually this picture will change, and he may feel he has the power actually to fly over the abyss: with light streaming around him and with a feeling of deepest happiness he soars across the yawning gap. Such pictures indicate that the ether-body is beginning to loosen or is already loosened, and that it is coming to have experiences without the aid of the physical body. Without this we cannot but feel at first that we have lost all firm ground from under our feet, and so there arises the whole *mise-en-scène* of the abyss.

What is the significance of this stage of development in the interplay of our members as regards our capacity for superphysical perception? Consider a person whose ether-body is still firmly bound up with his physical body, at a time when his astral body is engaged in perception, whether of the outside or the interior world. Now the only thing that gives him any awareness at all of the astral body's experiences is the close connection which this sets up with the physical and etheric bodies during waking-hours, whereby it receives what may be called a mirror-reflection of its perceptions. This connection is interrupted during deep sleep, as is also therefore all consciousness of what the astral body is perceiving. We might compare our waking experience to the awareness we get, say, of a wall by colliding with it. If such a collision actually occurred through some movement of ours when we were asleep, and our astral body were already sufficiently involved with the physical-etheric body lying in the bed, we would in fact wake up and be aware of the wall. If on the other hand the astral body had not yet joined forces with the physical as well as the etheric body, the event would be mirrored only in the ether-body and a series of pictures would be seen. If the astral body had been purified, become selfless, the pictures would be free of anything deriving from the lower, merely personal ego, and would tell us something of significance about the physical object or the spiritual being upon which the astral body had made impact. Correct training can impart the ability to assume the inner attitude at will whereby the ether-body is loosened even in the waking day-consciousness. If the higher man in us—and in the first place this means the perceiving astral body— manages, so to say, to face towards whatever is the object of research, then he will 'touch' the being sought. Such an experience will then not be reflected in the physical organs but in the ether-body alone, and the investigator will have a picture-perception of an angel, maybe, or of one of the elementary beings of Nature. But these initial experiences are *reflections, pictures* in the truest sense of the word, and must not be taken for the real beings as such. One and the same angel may reflect itself into our consciousness on one occasion as a quite small, delicately formed picture, and as a huge figure filling the whole landscape on another. It all depends on the degree to which our ether-body has expanded. And the purer and so truer these reflections, the more delicate will be their colours to begin with. Rudolf Steiner once referred to the very delicacy of these colours as indicating that one has to do with a true, relevant body-free experience of the kind to which modern spiritual schooling leads. These reflections are often so impalpable that modern man, accustomed as he is to garish sense-impressions, is in danger of sleeping through them. This is no doubt how we can understand Rudolf Steiner's remark: 'The young people are already standing in the spirit; there is only the danger that they will sleep through it'.*

Thus the first change the student experiences in spiritual training is a loosening of the ether-body, which can go so far that he feels himself expanding into the universe and that he attains a view of the cosmos based on personal experience and not merely on theory; it will certainly differ from the universe of Copernicus.

There must be no question of attempting such an expansion of the ether-body without at the same time making the utmost effort to purify and give form to the sentient body and to imbue one's whole feeling for the world and other human beings with the reality of the Christ-Impulse. Otherwise the reflections in the ether-body will represent not only spiritual truths but also purely personal features of the soul, or when interpreted range themselves around the personality in a completely subjective way. It would then be as if one were to dress up as a priest, a general or a judge and inflate one's ego by imagining that with the clothes one had also assumed the powers of office! It would be only too easy for personal desires, wishful thought about oneself and one's previous incarnations, negative attitudes to the world around, and other such contents of the unpurified astral body to be reflected in the ether-body in the outer guise of spiritual experiences. It is to such illusions and self-deceptions that the unpurified soul exposes itself before the mirroring ether-body, instead of attaining through its own gradual catharsis to a sight of the heavens opening and, as it says in John 1.51, of 'the angels of God ascending and descending upon the Son of man'.

Here we have the reason why it is and always has been a condition of any spiritual schooling that the soul powers must be harmonized and the astral body purified. As the ancient mysteries drew to their close in times already historical, it became extremely difficult to lead all but a few souls to an ordered experience of the spiritual world, and a preparation over many long years was required. We know that Pythagoras for example took decades to make his way through the Oriental centres of occult schooling before embarking on his own activity as a spiritual leader. Later on, notably towards the end of the second century A.D., when the ancient initiation-knowledge was in full decline, the attempt was nevertheless sometimes made to give a candidate if but a single glimpse of the spiritual world, to enable him for instance to get an insight into his own destiny; the priests would contrive brief but terrifying purification-episodes that so shook the candidate that at any rate for the occasion his lower nature was as if totally melted out of him. Pausanias has something to say about such 'purifications' in his description of the oracle of Trophonius.*

Now the time came in the development of humanity when all men were to be in a position to turn to the spirit, to the kingdom of heaven, and when it was to be left to the freedom of each individual, moreover, to travel this path even without guidance from a centre of initiation. Christ made this possible by His life on earth and by His death. He not only healed and sanctified those He met in Palestine, but enabled the whole body of the earth, the whole of humanity to take part in this healing and sanctification for all days to come. The earth-consecrating life of Christ is engraved so deeply into the spiritual sphere that it can be experienced by any soul that raises itself up to spiritual insight, even if it has never heard anything of the physical events that took place in Palestine. At the time of Christ's earthly life mankind was approaching its nadir, its most extreme separation from the spirit, and there was the great danger that such a redemptive spiritual experience would not be accessible for ages to come, so that the consequences for mankind of Christ's intervention would be correspondingly deferred. Therefore the life of Christ was recorded in writing in several versions, which were handed down to posterity in the Gospels as the story of what took place. Rudolf Steiner has told us the reasons for the discrepancies between them, and at the same time shown why the Gospel of St. John can be a particular aid in raising the soul to the spirit: it is written in such a way that anyone who completely absorbs himself in it experiences such a purification of his soul-body, that he thereby makes the ground ready for taking Christ up into himself.

The spiritual process which enabled the 'beloved disciple' to compose his Gospel with such power is indicated, as Rudolf Steiner says, in the words of Christ from the cross: 'Woman, behold thy son! . . . Behold thy mother!'

Before considering further details of St. John's Gospel, let us examine more closely this clue which Rudolf Steiner gave in the above-mentioned lecture from the cycle on this Gospel.[9] From the total context of the picture-language of the Mysteries we become aware that Christ spoke those words in the exalted language which addresses not man's intellect but that part of his soul which is capable of grasping a spiritual content in pictures.

The soul-body of a man, the link between his physical body and the spirit, has always been experienced in the picture of a female being and was so represented in the visual and the narrative arts. The downfall and purification of what was thus figured has been the content of fairy tales, legends, myths and mystery-plays of all ages. Thus we find in the late Roman period, again about the second century, woven as a story into a novel by Lucius Apuleius—a novel that taken by itself gives a telling enough picture of the ethical decline of that century—the well-known tale of Amor and Psyche. Now *psyche* is Greek for soul and *amor* is Latin for love. Love is the purest and highest activity of man's true ego, and this is the noble sense, far above the philandering which other classical sources make play with, in which Apuleius portrays his Amor. He gives an account of Psyche's arduous way of purification, describing all her trials and tribulations, until she can unite with Amor not only in sleep as before, that is without conscious recognition, but consciously in the pure spiritual world.

This tale is the last reminiscence of an initiation-myth about the purification or *catharsis* of the human soul. We find it in metamorphoses in the tales of nearly all peoples. It is the story of the princess doomed to unite with a monster, who however enters her presence each night unseen in a wonderful change of form. She is told she must never try actually to set eyes on him, but ignoring the warning, she lights a lamp whose oil drips on the princely being sleeping beside her; instead of being released from his spell he must leave her. She goes in search of him through many trials, and after hardships without number she is at last able to break his spell and to unite with him in his true shape. (Here the ego is no longer represented in its divine form but in its enchantment within matter, which can only be broken by the purification of the soul.)

The woman who unites with a god and undergoes severe trials before giving birth to the hero who forms and redeems mankind, Heracles for example, is in classical mythology the customary picture of the human soul as it struggles for purification, and conceiving through the spirit, brings forth the higher man out of itself.

Sorrow and pain transformed into a purified and active life-capacity is called wisdom, *sophia*. In the ancient schools of wisdom the purified astral body was called the Virgin Sophia. From the farthest East to the extreme West we find this picture in hieratic art, be it Isis of the Egyptians with Horus at her breast, or the Celtic *virgo paritura*, the virgin who will give birth, over whose underground mystery-vault the Gothic Christians built Chartres cathedral. With their much

more direct experience of religious realities than we are accustomed
to, they had no trouble in accepting the virgin goddess of the Celts
with the sun-child on her knees as a representation of the mother of
Christ, and to worship her accordingly. This brings before us the
deeper connection between the legendary figures of the ancients and
the mother of the Saviour, as indeed we can see from Rudolf Steiner's
Christology, which makes plain that the earthly path of Jesus Christ
was a physical living-through of the most profound initiation mysteries. His physical life was a picture of the spiritual life in terms of
reality. And for the one disciple who, like John, was called on to describe the spiritual aspect of the life of Christ, Christ's mother became identical with the Virgin Sophia who gives birth to the Son of
Man. The mother of Christ is to him the earthly image of the completely purified astral body, the bearer of the utterly spiritualized
power of Christ. It is the human soul in which Christ lives.

Now we read in St. John's Gospel that at Christ's words 'Behold
thy son . . . Behold thy mother!' . . . 'from that hour that disciple
took her unto his own: εἰς τὰ ἴδια (eis ta idia)' means: into the own,
or into his own property or possession, into that which belongs to
the ego. In the knowledge of what the ideal form of the pure mother
implied in ancient times, these words are filled with quite a special
meaning: they bear the stamp of a deep initiation-process. This astral
body, given power by the spirit and irradiated by Christ, whose earthly picture is the figure of the mother standing under the cross, the
Teacher unites with his pupil. From now on John has this astral
body; he accepts it as his own. And out of the forces of this astral
body he can record the life of his Master according to its *spiritual*
relationships. Because this life has been put into words in such a way,
a force is in them which can set that going in the reader which will
lead him in the same direction, towards the same source, out of which
they have themselves been written.

Christ has opened the new way, the way of the free, peace-filled ego.
He has opened it to us through His life on earth. But He has also
given a help to anyone wishing to model his life after His own, for
He made it possible for one of the Gospels to shape the soul in such
a way that it can carry the pure divine ego in itself. The importance
of St. John's Gospel for mankind lies in the purifying influence the
study of it exerts on the astral body: the Gospel according to St. John
creates in us the Virgin Sophia.

The Significance of
St. John's Gospel for Spiritual
Development Today

St. John's Gospel holds a special position among the four gospels. Its symbol is the eagle, which rises up into the luminous heights of divine wisdom. The spiritual eagle-forces radiate through man from out of his head-region. The eagle of St. John's Gospel can be a picture for us of these head-forces as they soar up into the heights of divine wisdom to where they can perceive the Logos, the creative Word-forces of the universe (see page 27). What this implies tells us why it is particularly the Gospel of St. John which lays hold with such powerful effect on so many souls today. For we are living at a time when these human head-forces, as soon as they are able to follow their own true nature, are seeking the way up, however hard, from out of the sphere of materialistic thought into that of the spirit. On the other hand mankind is standing nearer in consciousness than ever before to that threshold which leads into the pre-natal sphere. And this has the closest possible connection with the revival now beginning of the living word-forces in man, with an awakening of a heart-experienced insight into everything that lives in the word.

While this as it were is the subsoil, the ground out of which this profound feeling for St. John's Gospel grows, what calls it forth with such power is the goal towards which this gospel beckons the soul forward.

What is this goal? It is the development of the second, the higher man in us, the birth of what the Gospels call the *Son of Man*; for we have to do here in fact with the birth of the Son of Man, a birth which takes place when our ego has purified its sheaths and unites with Christ. This is what happened in the disciple whom the Lord loved, and it is in this sense that St. John's Gospel is a record of the teaching of Christ.

And it is in fact this Son of Man whom men these days are longing for in their heart of hearts. They are in search of their true, their higher ego with a vigour and intensity beyond anything of the sort in the nineteenth century. Now this yearning takes on various forms, various guises. Anyone unable to come to some clear understanding of what he is looking for will perforce manufacture an ideal that takes its features from a past he has either experienced himself or has learnt about; he will draw, that is, on his own past life or on history. In this latter event, he will find the hero to be followed in a Goethe, or maybe even in a Caesar or Napoleon; or he may turn from these or similar eminences to some altogether questionable individual whom only the perverted tastes of today could recommend. Whatever the choice, in tuning themselves to the character admired—its attributes are always sharply defined—the forces of the soul direct their endeavours and shape themselves accordingly. The truth of the matter, however, is that modern man is looking for his own higher being, he is longing to act out of the fully conscious power of his higher ego, to disentangle himself from the subjectivities of a petty, mistaken individualism, and in union with the great eternal laws to steer his life-endeavour towards the highest goals of mankind. This lay behind the unceasing search for a leader, for a hero and an ideal in the Youth Movement of the early twentieth century, but because no one ever became aware of this, no hero kept his place for long and no real guidance was discovered.

Let us consider the construction of St. John's Gospel from this aspect. The first words speak of the Logos-power of the divine cosmos. It is the light, the life of the world, and to the law of Moses it added love; it gives earthly men the power to become the sons of God. The whole of St. John's Gospel is concentrated in these few introductory sentences which embrace all cosmic and human evolution.

John the Baptist has a vision of this Logos-power entering the body of Jesus of Nazareth, when he sees Jesus approaching to be baptized in the Jordan: 'I saw the Spirit descending from heaven like a dove, and it abode upon him . . . the same is he which baptizeth with the Holy Ghost' (1.32 and 33).

The next sign follows immediately, when Christ meets His first disciples, and at this His very first meeting with them reveals to Simon his true, spiritual name: 'Thou shalt be called Cephas, which is by interpretation, A stone'. The spiritual truth of his higher man is disclosed to Simon at the sound of his true name. Nathanael, at his first meeting with Christ, is told the initiation-stage of inner development he has himself reached. 'Behold an Israelite indeed,' which means:

On your path of initiation you have attained union with your Folk-spirit. But this is not all: in the spirit Christ had perceived Nathanael's innermost being when it was in the state of enlightenment. The picture for this condition is that of sitting beneath the tree through which spiritual forces are flowing upwards from the depths to the divine heights and down again, embracing the one sitting under it. Accordingly Christ says: 'I saw thee under the fig tree.'

Those baptized by John went through a death-like experience at the moment of immersion and accordingly saw the entire panorama of their own life. Their ether-body was loosened for a few moments and their inner eye thus enabled to glimpse their own erstwhile existence with God and their own subsequent life on earth; they saw what had become of themselves through their own life and deeds since birth. That was the baptism by water, which loosened the ether-body. But a meeting with Christ did more than this: it liberated the spirit of a man, his kernel of fire; the meetings already referred to show this clearly. He opened His pupils' eyes to their higher being, which they had henceforth to draw into their conscious life; and this was to be the goal of their inner path. This is the baptism with the Holy Ghost. So the first chapter closes with the words: 'Jesus answered and said unto him, Because I said unto thee, I saw thee under the fig tree, believest thou? thou shalt see greater things than these. And he saith unto him, Verily, verily, I say unto you, Hereafter ye shall see heaven open, and the angels of God ascending and descending upon the Son of man.' In radiant pictures from life the disciples were introduced to us at the beginning of this chapter, and now, in these words of Christ's, there shines towards us the goal towards which He leads them and all mankind. It is the second man in us, the Son of Man, who is also a son of the heavens; the messengers of God, the hierarchies, can join company with him, can descend upon him from the heavens and ascend from him back to the spirit. Thus man is to be established as the lowest of the hierarchies, at the highest stage of development, that is, which he can attain as an earthly being, and he will mount towards it as he becomes ever more fully aware of what he is called to in the divine cosmic order.

If this goal is to be reached, the human ego will first have to cast off the bonds which confine it within blood-determined family connections, within a group-soul that holds it back from individual development. And so we see Christ first turning to Galilee whose people are despised as a mongrel community by the Jews. Just because of this, however, because they are less hampered by a bodily descent, their egos are readier for the spirit and more receptive for the Christ-Impulse than the Jews themselves. That is why Christ could turn water into wine at the wedding in Cana, teach a woman of Samaria and heal a nobleman's son (chapter 4).

In the picture-language of the Gospel, Christ's next deed is the purging of the temple. This physically real event is, like most others in the Gospels, at the same time an enlightening imagination wherein Christ teaches through His deed: the money-changers and merchants are driven out of the temple, the abode of the Divine Being. In the picture of the temple we can see the human body which has become the dwelling-place of passions and desires: they must be driven out of the temple of the body.

And the third chapter clearly says what must be done to reach this great goal: the birth of the higher man. This happens in Christ's conversation with the Pharisee named Nicodemus, to whom reference is made as a ruler of the Jews, which indicates that he is one of those who have reached a certain degree of spiritual capacity. And when we are expressly told that he 'came to Jesus by night', this means that he met Christ in a body-free condition.* Jesus says to him: 'Except a man be born from above, he cannot see the world of the spirit.' Luther translated this as 'born again'. The original expression is ἄνωθεν γενέθη (ánōthen genéthē), and we must go back to the original for a proper understanding of such a passage. The fundamental meaning of ἄνωθεν is first of all a spatial one, *from above*. That is the sense in which it was used by the Greek-speaking peoples, eventually also in the derived sense *down from the heights, from Heaven*. The Latin text already has the term *denuo* meaning *anew* or *again*, and Luther adopted that reading and translated it accordingly (the correct Latin should have been *desuper*);** this obscures the original meaning, to which, however, one must refer in the case of a document like the Gospel; it will make the words come alive. And alive they must become, if the scriptures are not to remain silent.

Once we have understood the basic meaning of ἄνωθεν we can perceive that a contrast is being made between the physical birth from below, from the elements of earth and water, and the birth of the spiritual man, of the Son of Man, from above. Not until He is born in us will our eyes be opened to the spiritual world. For this there is needed a consciousness not only of one's physical body but of one's own higher sheaths as well; these also must be purified. The elementary vehicles of the etheric and astral principles are water and air, and therefore Christ goes on to say, in the original meaning: 'Except a man be born of water and air [Greek: *pneuma**], he cannot enter the kingdom of God.' These members must also be born into the consciousness, or the Son of Man cannot take up His dwelling in our body.

So it is that this higher man is placed before us as a goal at the very beginning of St. John's Gospel. And the following chapters can be approached as the expression, in a language of great and profound pictures of life, of the purification of man as he lives in the water element of the formative forces and in the air element of the soul. In these two worlds, the etheric and the astral, Christ is the leader of seeking men. A series of pictures represents the healing and the evolution of the ether-body up to an understanding of the spiritual: the healing of the man infirm for 38 years, the feeding of the five thousand, and the walking on the sea. And after these events there sound forth the words of Christ: 'He that believes on me, out of his body will flow rivers of living water' (7.38). Christ is lord over the water of life, of the ether-world.

In chapter 8 the picture of the adulteress illustrates the working of sin in the astral body which has succumbed to the temptation of Lucifer. The following comment may be made at this juncture. In St. John's Gospel we can discern a specific principle of construction that is consistently observed in a most marvellous way. We are shown a picture that is firmly rooted in life and which can definitely be taken as the record of a real event: the wedding . . . the woman of Samaria . . . the nobleman . . . and now the adulteress. Christ enters upon the scene each time with some deed that gives active expression to His teaching. More than once He then turns to His disciples and to the educated Jews and goes into the significance of what He has done. This can be seen particularly clearly in chapter 8: first there is the confrontation with the woman who has sinned: 'I condemn thee not: go, and sin no more.' This Christ says after He has written on the ground, written into the body of the earth itself. But then He turns to His disciples and says: 'I am the light of the world.' In the language of spiritual science the astral body is also called the body of light. It is the human member that came particularly under the influence of Lucifer, the Light-bearer, and was thus drawn down into the world of the senses. But the true bearer of light is Christ, Who as the divine light pervades the whole world. It is He Who heals and sets free from death and sin. This healing and liberation of the astral body through the Christ-Light of the world is the content of the picture of the adulteress and the discourse following it in the 8th chapter.

Chapter 9 gives a synopsis of the developments attained so far in the picture of the man whose physical and spiritual eyes are opened, so that he believes in Christ. 'I am come into the world, that they which see not might see . . .'

And immediately before the 11th chapter, which describes the true birth of the higher man in the development and destiny of Lazarus, Christ says about Himself: 'I am the door.' The path of purification and development of the higher man, as described in the Gospel, has itself reached the door, as it were, the threshold that Lazarus now crosses by going through full initiation during the sleep of death. As one awakened, developed into his higher being, the disciple now listens to the further discourses of Christ.

These discourses give the disciples a new aim in the commandment concerning the purified power of the ego: 'Love one another as I have loved you' (13.34). These words embrace cosmic aims for the future, the whole development of ego-power. It is not the aggressive, self-assertive ego that is in view, but the ego that bestows, whose power flows out of its union with Christ: 'Love one another; as I have loved you, that ye also love one another.' Through His love for them, Christ thus lets stream into His pupils a force they are now to live out of and make effective in their own deeds. To love Christ means to become united with His aims;* it means to serve the development of the world in His name, out of the forces of His being. Therefore the result of this development is described as a power that the pupil of Christ will possess: 'And whatsoever ye shall ask in my name, that I will do' (14.13). That is the *wish-power* of which the German mystic Heinrich Suso speaks and which is in a certain sense the fruit of the highest spiritual development. Suso treats of it in the 32nd chapter of his own life-story. The soul inquires what God gives to those who struggle spiritually towards the highest goal. The answer is that at the highest stage of all God gives them the three gifts of wish-power, peace, and union with God. This wish-power is to be understood in the sense that the human being has struggled through to a grasp of the cosmic laws that flow creatively through the world out of the being of God, so that all the wishes he has arising out of such a union cannot but be in harmony with these laws. Thus the wishing of anyone who has come so far is in reality a willing that is also a knowing of what is necessary; it is an active knowing that is creative, that is able to bring an event about because it is in line with the forces of the true cosmic order. That is 'wish-power'. And in the sense of St. John's Gospel it means asking for something in the name of Christ.

Christ's farewell discourses that now follow lead into the deepest mysteries of spiritual and cosmic relationships. The disciple whom the Lord loves hears them in the spirit: at the Last Supper he is leaning on his Master's bosom. And his being travels the path so far that beneath the cross under which the redemptive consecration of the earth is being completed he can receive the mother of the Lord, the Virgin Sophia.

He is at the end of his own path, and after his Master's death on the cross he can see His being within the earth's sphere of life. He has won the power to write down the story of his path in the Gospel, the good tidings, as a help to future mankind.

This Gospel therefore follows the whole path up to the birth of the second man in us, as he frees himself of the blood-bonds of physical ancestry and passes through all the stages of purification proper to each sheath, until he unites with Christ in the service of the world.

St. John's Gospel is the revelation of the Christ Logos-power. It also shows the way along which a man can unite with this power and thus attain the highest stage of development within his reach. It introduces us in the first place to the cosmic aspect of the Logos; it goes on to tell how the Logos reveals Itself first to the spiritual eye of John the Baptist at the Jordan and then to the first disciples. And now in pictures of earthly life there is described the path that was followed by the Christ-Being in His once-for-all incarnation on the earth as man. It is at the same time also the path of His disciple John, who together with Christ his Master walked the path of initiation that can still be trodden by every man today. This scripture shows mankind the path of truth to the life in the spirit.

The Word

'Whence comest thou?'—'From the chasms where the gold dwells,' said the Snake.—'What is grander than gold?' enquired the King.— 'Light,' replied the Snake.—'What is more quickening than light?' said he.—'Conversation,' answered she.

What is more quickening than light? Conversation! These words from Goethe's Fairy Tale are a door to the great spiritual realities the narrative conceals as an open secret; they can lead us into the deeper background of this tale. Goethe places before us pictures, pictures that are a kind of script for spiritual facts. Just as the written word expresses events, facts, the essentials of any being or deed, so behind the tapestry of this story there is another world, the world of spiritual forces that emanate from spiritual beings.

And the words: 'What is more quickening than light?—Conversation' are, as I have said, a door to this world that borders on the physical.

Out of the chasms where the gold dwells rises the Snake. This is a picture out of the spiritual sphere into which the creative artist Goethe ascended in his search for spiritual insight. It is a region of the devachanic world,* the world in which the inside and outside of creation change places. The mineral, rock-like formations of one's own head, the convolutions of the human brain are spread before the seer like a landscape with rocks and crevasses in which what is alive in man glides about in the ego-like form of the Green Snake. In these clefts within the human organ of thinking dwells the gold of wisdom, the wisdom the Green Snake needs as food in order to attain enlightenment.

Wisdom in the human sphere is a formative force, whereas the formative force in the spiritual region is light. Light is grander than gold because it is more spiritual.

Wisdom Weaves in Light

The primal polar opposite to the light as forming-force is life. The
region of life is closed to man: only within the line of bodily descent
can he out of his own being produce a being of like nature; he cannot interfere with the generative line of other living beings and create
something new. Only divine beings can do that. But man, the tenth
hierarchy, is striving and struggling along the path of his development towards the higher beings. If he cannot find the seed of all-
embracing creativity in the generative pole of his being, he can do so
in his own middle realm, where in his own body there meet together
form and life, or as one could also say, wisdom and love, above and
below: he sends the power of his breath into his larynx and forms the
word. The word is the higher creative pole of man—it is the creative
organ of divine beings: 'In the beginning was the Word.'

In times past there were on earth centres where men were guided
in such a way that at least a few could preserve the knowledge of the
higher worlds, of the higher powers latent in man, while the general
run of humanity made their evolutionary descent into material existence. In such centres men were initiated into the mysteries, into the
creative power of the Word. Rudolf Steiner* tells how when the old
wisdom was still alive at Ephesus, the aspirant was received there
with the greeting:

> O man, speak, and thou
> revealest through thyself
> world-becoming.

And when he was dismissed, the farewell sounded:

> World-becoming revealeth itself
> through thee, O man,
> when thou speakest.

And Rudolf Steiner points out that in every word formed by man the
element of fire, of warmth, flows upwards and the moist, water-
element downwards, while the air-element is formatively at work in
between.

What does Rudolf Steiner want to show us through this? He is
disclosing to contemporary mankind the mystery of how our cosmic
system was born, how the body of warmth on Ancient Saturn was

first formed, how the rudiments of the air-element were established
on Ancient Sun and those of the moist element on Ancient Moon,
and how at last the physical earth-element was created during the
evolution of the Earth.

This is the macrocosmic mystery to which the Ephesian aspirant's
attention was drawn by his instruction in the microcosmic creative
power of the human word. In every word man reveals world-becom-
ing, the passage of creation through the harmony of the warm, the
aeriform and the moist. But our word cannot also create a body for
itself out of the fourth element of earth, because man does not yet
hold sway over life in the earth. His word works etherically, and to
the measure in which he commands the etheric laws of what flows
from him as sound out of the larynx and makes them his own, will he
come ever closer to a sovereignty over life itself; for these ether-forms
of his creation, on the current of which the fire of his goodwill or
malevolence flows from him, can sound in creative harmony with the
laws of the ether, with the life-conditions of the other realms of
Nature. No one at present can remodel the physical shapes of Nature
through the forming power of his word, but a person capable of intense concentration can certainly do this with what is still etheric,
namely the fluidic and warming elements.

This is only a first tender beginning of man's recovery of the
creative power of the Logos, of creation through the Word. Grouped
around the human larynx are the parathyroid glands; they are ar-
ranged square-wise, that is according to the archetypal form of life,
and out of them there will one day stream forth the four kinds of
ether.* Today man is standing before a world of creative life, which
in primeval times he ruled as a magus of the Word and out of which
he found himself driven through the corruption of his desires. The
gate into this world is still closed against him, but Rudolf Steiner has
shown how the heavy bolts can be drawn back; he has given everything the striving man needs for re-entering the realms of life.

What one day will stream out of human speaking with fully conscious power is already present in its beginnings; for according to the
mood that goes with it it can work into the feelings and through them
into the other's sphere of etheric life, either to help or to hurt. And
so when a man is in talk with another and, far from feeling 'I' only
egoistically, lets his words harmonize through his 'you'-feeling with
those of the other, the result is life-kindling, it is in the sense of the

Fairy-Tale 'quickening'. When in conversing, therefore, they set aside the merely personal, two human beings can build up something in which life is at work. Though one man alone cannot as yet command the life-forces by the power of his word, two certainly can build together through theirs, they can awaken life; there must only be present between them through their feeling towards each other the purified ego-force, the divine ego-bearer.

Thus speech between men is truly more quickening than light, than light which is present in thinking, in wisdom and in the realm of forms.

> Wisdom weaves in the Light,
> Life works in the Word.

Behind the wisdom-enwoven, radiant picture-realm of Goethe's Fairy Tale there surges the ever-active world of life-forces in all their reality, and these find their way into the world of man in the sounding of the word, and in the sounding word seek their passage by way of man into the realms of Nature herself.

On Love

As we learn to distinguish more and more between our own sheaths, we realize that we cannot speak of love in general. Love is lived by way of the individual sheaths: it is they that form the link with the other person, and they which therefore determine the dynamic quality of the love. Most of us will find the one or the other sheath predominating in our love. Love that lives in balanced harmony throughout a person's whole being will, like all harmony today, be very difficult to achieve. In the sense of Greek wisdom it may appear as *prokopé* (in progress, in thriving) but not nearly yet as arrived at *tèlos* (the goal).

And so there is, besides physical love, love expressed primarily through the ether-body, love that uses the astral body, and love for which the ego is the instrument. But the latter is likely to remain somewhat abstract at a time when the magical powers of the ego have hardly begun to unfold. The ego will not be able to practise love until in the course of the evolution of human culture it has fully developed itself and has transformed the sheaths into pliable instruments under its own complete control.

Love lies more in the ether-body of persons whose astral body is in some way not fully developed. Such love has, so to speak, a suctional quality about it in that the loving subject would draw its object into its own sphere of life and like a loving 'cosmos' impose its etheric law on the other person. This leads to all kinds of complications. The ether-body is the seat of our habits and permanent traits of character. Such an ether-love runs the danger of bringing these features into violent conflict unless the two persons concerned have or can develop inclinations and habits that completely coincide. Temperament is here a mutually important factor: unless one dominates over the other entirely, the two may clash, or they may depress each other severely. When the two persons live together, for example as a married couple, this becomes noticeable as the cause of enervating family rows that are not made any easier by the fact that the two souls are usually linked by some real karmic connections. Once the colourful blossoming of such love has passed, it is only the leaves that grow uneventfully on and on . . . or at least would like to do so . . . and there pre-eminently we have the etheric at work.

It will be a different matter if the astral body is intensely activated in such feelings. One should really manage to use the astral body not only as a nervous feeler that shrinks back in antipathy as soon as it touches or is touched by anything not entirely in conformity with itself: it ought to be developed into a proper sense-organ that remains calm even if the other being is felt to be strange to its own nature at first. That is the only way to get to know the other person at any real depth: for only in that case will the body of light of the one astral body shine like a sun into the other and discover its brighter side. Then the deepest secrets can be disclosed to those beholding each other in a sphere of light.

Love with the ether-body is cumbersome: a man would have to be at an advanced stage of development to use his ether-body with sufficient mobility to loosen what binds him to it and to himself. But the astral body is more nimble by nature, very nimble indeed: it can leave its physical foundation more easily and become immersed in another being; it does not suck and cling but it sounds—and listens to what is also sounding. It sips at the cup of the other flower, finding the sweetest and most delicate nectar—or maybe poison. . . . But it must strive to become an alert organ of perception, not only for what is finished in the other person but for its past and for its future possibilities. Then it will discover the other's inner architecture, which may be very different from the external appearance.

An astral body that learns not to recoil, hurt and offended, from an experience but to stay quite calm within it, even if it is painful, will also work on further with it at night, when it is not so impeded by the physical body. This is the time when ever deeper secrets of that experience are discovered. But this calm, this keeping still which corresponds to an absolute reality of union between the astral body and the object of its knowledge, has a special effect on this object also, on the other person—purely in the sphere of the soul and spirit. The beneficial, harmonizing results will flow back in a rich stream sooner or later. For in this calm act of knowledge the egos act on each other on a higher plane.

There is one condition necessary for such an experience: inner silence. Complaint and prattle about such experiences to others, to a third person, will cause the sublimity of it to vanish—as if a surface on which the most delicate figures were beginning to form out of gold dust were hammered on with the fist.

Metamorphoses

As dusk falls over the meadow, the snow is melting. Fruit-trees all spaced out stand there dark on the white surface. Although the sun is no longer shining, the snow is still melting. We can hear how the earth is taking in and swallowing the trickles of water. There is a singing and a ringing of gentle bell-like sounds over the whole expanse of this patch of earth.—The meadow is rejoicing.—Around the trees and bushes the snow is melting more quickly: the plants are beginning to take up warmth, and so the snow is melting much faster near them than elsewhere. At this time of the melting snow we can particularly experience how the light and warmth descending from above call forth the surging life that is awakening in the depths of the earth.

In these days just before spring, Nature goes through its greatest metamorphosis: the life of the plant is beginning to unfold in the seed. The archetypal forms of the individual plants are shaping and building their physical appearance. This does not remain rigid like the wonderfully shaped-out crystal but keeps on transforming itself from seed to shoot; from stem to leaf, to flower, and so to the fruit. The plants are alive!

If we try to think this metamorphosis ahead of the visible form, and consider the plant when still in the seed, we arrive at a state of existence which physical sight cannot perceive. The forces that are going to form the plant are already present in the living seed, and the spiritual eye can see them as billowing colours of light around it.

Spring in particular is the time to experience this transition from the plant's potential state to the fully developed form accessible to our physical senses. The cold of winter had seized on the moisture in the blue-dark depths of the earth, forcing it from the watery into the rigid earth-condition, freezing it into the earth's body so that it was quite estranged from its own world of life. And now cosmic warmth and light flow down to earth again from the sun with increasing

61

power. Between the universe and the earth there begins that exchange of forces that manifests itself in metamorphoses: the warmth and the light melt the ice so that the water soaks into the earth, dissolving its substances and taking them up into its own fluidic element; they leave their state of rest and come into motion, they become transformable, so that they can flow from the mineral realm into that of the plants, from the region of death into the region of life.

The empathetic experience of this metamorphosis of Nature rouses special forces in our souls, if we do not limit our observation to the changes our eyes can see in the unfolding leaves and flowers but become sensitive also to the flow of warmth and moisture around the shoots and buds; if we develop a feeling for the life-bearing forces that are flooding the whole surface of the earth, then the earth's ether-weaving will awaken something in our own ether-body. This something is related to a strengthened power of memory, and as a play of forces in our own ether-body it begets in us a quite special experience, an ability to observe metamorphoses in human life itself.

First of all there is the great cycle of transformations along each individual's path of development, the transition from a purely spiritual existence to physical life on earth. The earth and the universe work together here also, when a human ego, ready for its task on earth, takes possession of the physical body prepared for it. Its body of light and warmth approaches union at birth with the physical body that is already pulsating with life and has been prepared for it on earth through the workings of destiny as the seed, the bud for its impending earthly activity.

This body of light and warmth is in particular the vehicle of a person's individuality. It has its being in the world of the spirit. And in its spiritual state it existed in tune with entirely different laws. The transformations are enormous which this spiritual being undergoes when it leaves the world of spirit to inhabit the world of matter.

If we are to kindle true spiritual life on earth, if the light that unceasingly incarnates from the spiritual into the earthly world is to win the victory and prevail, then we must gradually extend our consciousness to that world which is the home of the man of light and warmth, of the spiritual second man in us.

We have already seen that the present epoch, as the first phase of the Light-Age, stands out in human history becaues in it we are gradually beginning to perceive the forces coming down out of our home of light. The second man in us is entering our consciousness more and more. If we understand him, we can experience this human metamorphosis, or at least we can divine perhaps some gentle intimations of it. If human development is to continue in the right way, the oil must be lit in the earthly lamp in order to shed light and warmth on the deeds of men. The lamp must not be left standing empty and dark, while the oil wastes itself in flames elsewhere.

That is what we are struggling for. We must learn in full consciousness to unfold thoughts that are spiritually true, which are more and more able to build a bridge between the second man in us and our ordinary earth-conscious selves. Then these living thoughts will begin to kindle our soul-experience, and the great human task of our time, the metamorphosis of consciousness, will be carried through.

The second man in us had his own forms of experience, his own laws of life, before he embraced earthly existence. The memory of them lingers on in a child, but a child cannot raise them into consciousness. When the second man completely unites with the earthly man at puberty, this faint afterglow of spiritual existence usually dies away. It is the experience of the Fall of Man: the gates of Paradise close tight.

At the present juncture in history a leader was given mankind in Rudolf Steiner who could set going in its entirety the cultural renewal necessary to keep the second man alive in us beyond this point of death. The spiritual science Rudolf Steiner gave us as the fruit of his research can change our thinking and our experience completely. He gave to education the task of guiding the child in such a way as to foster the second man until the ego-consciousness in the growing human being can take him into its own hands.

The task of tending the young spiritual forces of our times requires us to become aware of the great metamorphoses in experience which the second man in us undergoes when he comes down to earth. When we do this, we realize that all anthroposophical indications for the forming of one's life and of oneself are nothing but the attempt to prepare in ourselves a home for the second man with his purely spiritual laws of life and to provide him with a field of action, so that light and warmth can be kindled in the earthly lamp.

The laws governing the existence of this spiritual man of light and warmth were very different before birth. This becomes evident when we consider that in the spiritual world before birth he was not con-

fined to a limited form but lived in a mighty effusion of being, in a
great diastole. We can approach the nature of this expansion in consciousness, this living in a world beyond time and space, if we succeed
in freeing ourselves from the body in the right way and are then able
in all certainty to say: Now you have quite overcome time and space.
In such a condition of inner awareness things at a distance from the
observer in space or time can now be perceived, because in the body-
free state the spiritual man alone is the cognitive agent, and for him
limits of form, space and time do not exist. Any lucid cognitive act
of our thinking is already a miniature image of the exact body-free
experience which involves inner vision and hearing, for in all such
cognition it is the spiritual man who is active, even though still within
his bodily prison. It is for this reason that our thinking offers us the
starting-point for a spiritual development appropriate to the present
time.

Thus indeed it is a mighty diastole the second man is living in before incarnation; the contraction, the systole follows at birth and
remains the second man's state of existence during his earthly life-
time. As the archetypal phenomenon therefore within the spiritual
existence of this being there hold sway the two forces of expansion
and contraction, of diastole and systole, which Goethe was the first
to discover in the etheric growth-region of the plant.

All Rudolf Steiner's descriptions of spiritual existence and of the
forms of experience obtaining in it show that in this polarity we really
have the two fundamental forces of the universe. He tells us how
spiritual beings lacking physical organs of sense have only the one
cognitional possibility, namely that of extending themselves into the
being they are seeking to know. This is the stage of knowledge on
man's path of spiritual development which Rudolf Steiner calls Intuition: it does not use the brain but the will as the organ, the power
of love as the working factor, in the act of cognition. And when such
a spiritual being wants to return into itself again, it must bring into
play a contracting force in order to disengage from the other being.
Evidently then, diastole and systole are the spiritual being's essential
life-activity: they are the play of forces fundamental to the non-
physical world. Goethe's great genius was the first to discover them,
in the border region where the spiritual is closest to the physical, the
ether-region of plant growth. But now that Rudolf Steiner has opened
up for us such a wealth of knowledge from the world of the spirit, we

can realize that systole and diastole are not only operative in the etheric growth-world of the plant; they are the archetypal forms of movement in all spiritual existence; they are the forms of life for the non-physical world as a whole.

And they are also present in the human soul. From the time that the life of the soul became an object of research, the multitude of emotions was found to root in the two basic feelings of pleasure and displeasure, joy and pain. What is going on when we are pleased? The astral body, the vehicle of our emotions, expands and sometimes even draws the ether-body along with it to a certain degree, so that our blood flows more to the surface, and we blush for joy and breathe more deeply: this is diastole. And when we feel pain the astral body contracts and can even get cramped into fear; our blood is pressed in towards the heart, we grow pale and cold: we experience systole. Joy and pain, the two basic feelings, can show us even without spiritual vision that they function by way of expansion and contraction. Not that this movement is recognizable physically, but we become aware of it at once when the astral body begins to exist in our thinking as a concept for the vehicle of the soul. They are fundamental dynamic phenomena of earthly man's emotional life, and in them we can see something like a miniature image of the play of forces governing us before birth. This gives us a basis of experience whereby we can understand in more than just an abstract way the life-form of a body-free being as described by Rudolf Steiner.

However, joy and pain are by no means to be understood as the metamorphosed result of pre-natal diastole and systole. The foregoing reflection was only meant to help us feel our way better into the previous description of pre-natal existence, for our feeling-life is that part of our soul in which diastole and systole most clearly appear in our life on earth.

Therefore we have still to ask in what way the great pulsatory rhythm of our spiritual existence, the ability to expand in knowledge and to contract into oneself again, is transformed into our earthly soul-life.

Rudolf Steiner stressed in this connection that an earthly birth corresponds to a heavenly death. Every death-process, however, liberates something spiritual, and only the form that served this as a foundation and instrument undergoes the actual death and becomes a corpse. It is the same here. The power active in the pre-natal cognitive

act was sympathy, the ability to *feel with* the object of knowledge; we call this pre-natal or living thinking. After birth our cognition is no longer based solely on sympathy, on love, for the force
of love is the spiritual element liberated from the process of knowing
by the spiritual death that corresponds to earthly birth, and is henceforth active only in our feeling and not in our thinking. It works as
the quality of sympathy in our experience of other people and of
Nature. Our love for human beings, the warm interest that draws us
to all the variety of Nature are the earthly remnant of our pre-natal
cognitive power of diastole. The corpse left over after that death
which men call birth, however, is our earthly thought, for in this
there no longer works the pre-natal power of love. The trace of sympathy in it has grown so small that it can only be called antipathy!
And the benumbed earthly thoughts can no longer encompass any
of the real spirituality present in whatever the world shows us. All
they have access to is the mineral element in the world of finished
form, which is as cold as they. Thus the pre-natal love-borne communion with spiritual beings, expressing itself in diastole, is on the
one hand metamorphosed on earth into compassion, fellow-feeling,
and on the other into dead thinking.

The pre-natal systole enables us eventually to contract to the extent of entering our physical body, and the power active in it is called
by Rudolf Steiner 'fear'. This is not the feeling usually so called: it
is more a contraction, a pulling away from, an antipathy against anything spiritual. When a person has moved for too long in very stimu-
lating, highly gifted company wants to retire for a while into reflective
privacy, he may even feel a slight aversion, a faint shock at an un-
expected meeting with one of his previous associates. In the same way
every human soul begins to fear, in this sense, the whole spiritual
world, heading rather towards its earthly existence in order to work
at itself through its own ego. This pre-natal fear is accordingly metamorphosed into another contracting force that we have at our command after birth: it turns into will, the power of soul which becomes
deed, and works formatively on itself and on the world. Our deeds
give us the sense of our ego, of our own personality, our self-ex-
perience, our self-feeling. Will and self-feeling are the earthly forces
resulting from the metamorphosis of pre-natal fear. If we could see
what each of our voluntary impulses looks like from the other side
of the Threshold, we could perceive behind it the contracting force

that was originally spiritual fear. The Guardian at the Threshold keeps this knowledge from coming into our consciousness on earth. But if we give a sensitive ear, so to speak, to our own volitions, we can become quite aware—provided we have attained the necessary inner truthfulness—that much that is done outwardly springs from an inner fear of the opposite to what is being attempted. (Obviously this fear may be altruistic or it may be purely egoistic; but that is a moral difference.)

We can now summarize this with Rudolf Steiner's own scheme:*

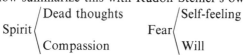

Thus we have in our earthly thought corpses of our pre-natal experience of cosmic thought. In our self-feeling and our will we have soul-forces that show distinct signs of systole, a contraction in the sense of a formative force which is the opposite to self-release and expansion. And compassion has kept its pre-natal nature to the greatest extent, preserving even in earthly life the ability to become immersed in another being, in another's feelings; it is the most personal and intimate element of all in the human soul. Every act of compassion contains something of the pre-natal, heavenly power of knowledge we had before we underwent the great metamorphosis into earthly existence, whereas that other part of our life-filled interweaving with cosmic thoughts was turned by birth into our dead abstract thinking, into earthly knowledge. The two kinds of knowledge, which we might call earthly and heavenly, are polar opposites, as are the regions they lead into; for the world of matter, of mineral, of anything dead is all that dead thinking gives us access to, while compassion transports us into veritable pastures of life—the life of the soul. Compassion is what we must practise in order to develop the organ of knowledge which alone will lead us to a knowledge of the second spiritual man in us, the cloud-like being that passes from one earthly life to another.

If we thus follow the great metamorphosis that the three powers of our soul undergo at the transition from pre-natal to earthly existence, we begin to realize that Rudolf Steiner's word that we have to turn selfless love into an organ of knowledge means exactly this: we must deliberately bring our pre-natal kind of cognition to life, for this is the only way in which the spiritual man in us can unfold on earth, and whilst still in an earthly body become active as knower within the spiritual world.

Compassion, fellow-feeling with the metamorphoses undergone by all things living: that is our way to develop these powers. We must unite the forces of our soul in quite an impersonal way with the processes of Nature, and in the experience of this, venture towards the cosmic forces that release rigid form into flowing life, unfolding a becoming in the realm of the become. This method of knowledge will enable twentieth-century man to overcome the rigidities every-where prevalent in his civilization and to work for its total renewal in co-operation with the creative, livingly transformative wisdom of the cosmos.

Consider Rudolf Steiner's advice in *Knowledge of the Higher Worlds.*[1] In the very first chapters he recommends that we turn to natural phenomena and observe minerals, plants, animals and human beings. Looking more closely, we see that he always draws our atten-tion to a transition, a particular change in the growth of the plant or in the feeling experienced by the animal or person observed. Other exercises make a comparison between two different realms of Nature, but again it is really a transition we have to do with, for example in the comparison between the flow of sap in a plant and the blood cir-culation of an animal. It is always an exercise in the perception of metamorphosis. But we are emphatically required to become one with the process in question, to feel our way into it, for without this sympathetic identification our soul-forces would take no turn towards development, since they would experience in the exercises nothing of that releasing enlargement that alone makes for supersensible knowl-edge. No matter how accurate the observation, if the soul remains cold there is furthered nothing but the intellect, dead thinking, earth-ly but never heavenly knowledge.

The time has now come for us also to kindle this feeling-with-the-other in our observation of Nature, so that we learn to see the ele-mentary world, which is the next behind the physical: it is the world of the formative forces, out of which we can advance to experience that of the forces of soul and spirit. Anthroposophy shows the modern way to this, but in the older cultural periods of mankind, when the human soul had not yet arrived at the nadir of its descent into the material world, the spiritual leaders of mankind tried to keep those pre-natal forces of compassion and fear alive in the souls while the descent was in progress. They did not use exercises such as Rudolf Steiner has now given us; at the time of the great annual feasts, human destinies were put before the soul in artistic form: they were enacted in the Greek drama. The mighty trilogies of Aeschylos and Sophocles, who still had some knowledge of the mysteries, gripped and shook the spectators' inmost being. These tragedies are by no means so evenly harmonious as the dramas in which other nations later on tried to imitate them. They are terrifying and often dripping with blood (think of Oedipus and Hecuba, to mention only two)—a modern person, thin-skinned and feeble-souled as he often is, is hard put to it to take them. But then they were deliberately intended to arouse fear and compassion, which were meant to grip the souls and loosen their relationship with the physical body. They are the two basic forces of pre-natal life, and in so strongly agitating the inner man, they kept the spirit in movement even though civilization was drawing humanity down into an ever deeper intimacy with the world of matter.

But these efforts on the part of wise leaders would not have been enough. Human deeds were insufficient to kindle enough of this pure, cognitive compassion which is called love, in the hardening hearts of men. The human spirit that laid down the laws of communal life grew increasingly adamant and severe. 'An eye for an eye, a tooth for a tooth': that became the vengeful penal directive. A truly social attitude among the people would never have come about if the heavenly cognitive power of love had not been implanted in the hearts of men by an exalted cosmic event. Not laws, but an exemplary life lived right in the midst of humanity: a divine being, the very leader of the spirits that call the heart of the universe, the sun, their home, took possession of a human body. Christ gave His disciples only one commandment: 'Love one another as I have loved you . . . By this shall all men know that ye are my disciples.' This commandment we understand in its all-comprehensive meaning for the remodelling of the human being, the metamorphosis of the human soul which was made possible by the deed of Christ, if we look at it in the light of what has been said above. A divine being—the Cosmic being of Love itself— underwent the same metamorphosis we undergo with every incarnation. In earthly life we have only a feeble glimmer as a last remnant of our pure-pre-natal cognitive love: this love now blazed forth from the Christ into Jesus of Nazareth. It shone through all He did on earth and radiated with full knowledge into His surroundings: 'And he saw the thoughts of their hearts and said . . .' we are told time and again. And Christ implanted this love in mankind when in the great Easter sacrifice He relinquished His blood and let it flow into the rigidifying, dying world of earth.

Just as ice when melted by cosmic warmth becomes as water the vehicle of life, carrying earthly matter upwards with formative power into the light against the forces of gravitation, so does Christ's blood of sacrifice become the bearer into freedom for the spiritual life of man. As it flowed down it began to shine out within the life-sphere of the body of the earth. Within the earthly realm the metamorphosis from death to spiritual life set in when the divine being of Love let His warmth of life and love descend like dew into the dark depths of human and earthly existence.

When the snow melts in the warmth of the spring sun and the plants begin to green and grow, we can witness the most delicate of processes, outwardly quite insignificant. But these subtle happenings in Nature whisper of that most exalted event that once took place between the earth and the universe, when the sun was at the same spring point of its annual path: they tell of the Easter Mystery, the mystery of releasing, redeeming love.

The Dynamics of the Human Life of Soul

In the previous chapter we saw how human existence is based on the polarity of systole and diastole, how for the spirit-man the systole of birth follows on the diastole of that pre-natal condition in which he is out-poured through the entirety of the spiritual world and its inhabitants. And furthermore we saw that to go the way of training pointed out to us by Rudolf Steiner and to come to an understanding and an active forming of the spiritual man within us, we needed to attain that sort of consciousness whose essential dynamic lies in systole and diastole, the forces prevailing in the life before birth. This means that we must revive our great pre-natal cosmic diastole in such a way as to reconcile it with the systole of our physical existence.

Let us now turn to the spiritual man as he lives in us during earthly life, and see how it is with him in his house, how he comports himself in the physical body. Let us do this however under the aspect of the dynamic activity, the inner spiritual movement that leads to the phenomenal form of man within the sense-world with which our ordinary consciousness is familiar.

The man of spirit in us has to leave this house of his at least once every twenty-four hours when he falls asleep. In the spiritual study of man this fact tells us that the astral body is closely bound up with the ego, and the ether-body with the physical body. Every night the sentient body and the ego expand so as to enter and perceive the world they once came out of, but there is no diastole of the etheric and physical bodies until death; then the one expands in its dissolution into the cosmos while the other disintegrates into the substance of the earth.

Regarded therefore from the dynamic spiritual aspect, sleeping and waking represent a diastole and systole of the astral body and the ego. In the systole of waking the spiritual man in us perceives, feels, knows and wills in the physical world, and for this the sentient body uses the sense organs as instruments of knowledge, and the ego the physical body as the tool of its willing. The more perfect these instruments, the more comprehensive will be the knowledge attainable of the earthly world.—During the diastole of sleep the spiritual man undergoes cosmic experiences. In human states of existence long past these experiences were of a sublime, inexhaustible richness. On Ancient Moon, for example, part of the ether-body was loosened as well, and in *Occult Science*[6] we are told: 'This combination of the astral and life-bodies was like a delicate and wonderful musical instrument, on whose strings the mysteries of the universe sounded.' This cosmic music, moreover, gave shape to the rest of the human being which, possessing no individual ego at that time, was formed directly by the Sun-spirits themselves. Now that the individual ego has taken possession of the body and of the earth in the fullest sense, however, sleep is steeped in oblivion. Nor shall we be able to bring the experiences of sleep into our daytime-consciousness until we have so developed the spiritual sense-organs latent in the astral body that they can join forces with our etheric centres in the right way.

This systole and diastole of the spiritual man in us is still in some degree connected as formerly to sun-processes: with all the freedom from cosmic rhythms man has acquired, on the whole he still does his sleeping at night; that is, when the sun is working upon him through the earth.

Thus in regard to the movement of the astral body and ego, sleeping and waking represent a diastole and systole, expansion and contraction. They are like the polarities of spiritual existence and earthly birth, in that the diastole of sleep leads into the world of the spirit (even if we are no longer aware of it now) and the systole of waking up takes us into the earthly world which is dominated by death.

Let us now consider from this aspect how the human sentient body and ego develop when they enter the earthly human organization.

In order to appreciate more clearly the special constitution of the human being, we may take another look at the plant. While each plant has its own physical and etheric bodies, its astral body and ego are part of the plant group-soul and only work from out the cosmos upon the single plant at certain times of the year. When they do so, it is in a way that reveals something of the total life of the plant species. In diastole and systole the plant shoots forth leaf, stalk, and leaf again, until it comes to blossom and fruit. This is where the group astral body enters from outside and holds back the growth that would otherwise go on and on, and tinges the petals with colour. It is just this colour, more than anything else in a plant, that speaks to our souls and makes us feel so differently about a bluebell, say, and an exuberant red peony. Moreover, at this stage of development, the element of warmth actually comes into play: the temperature of the flowers, as has been ascertained by measurement, is above that of the leaves, in some plants considerably so, and it is known that the fruit also is enveloped in a sheath of warmth as it grows and ripens.

The group astral body enters from outside; this we can understand if instead of looking at the flowering-process in a single plant isolated from its natural environment, we take account of the whole species and consider it as a single being. The reason we must do this is that the plant astral body belongs to the group-soul and has its existence on a higher plane than the physical. If, then, we look at a whole species, we can see how in due season the flowering-process is poured out, as it were, over all its single members. Think, say, of the apple-tree: within certain latitudes the apple as species is spread over the surface of the earth in countless exemplars. If anyone were to look down from a great height, intent on seeing nothing but this, he would make out a strange shape spread over the earth's surface, not all the time in one unbroken piece and yet discernible so to say as one great body: the physical and etheric body of the apple-tree as a plant species. When in our own locality there may still be snow and the buds are firmly closed, the apple-blossom will already be unfolding in the south and, surging through this great plant-body like a wave of colour and scent, be carried north by the advancing warmth of spring. More and more apple-trees are thus transformed with the rose-white of unfolding flowers, as the warmth of their own cosmic encompassing soul is breathed over them. Just as in a human being we sometimes see how the blood, mounting up from the heart, touches neck, cheeks and forehead in turn, so also is it with the blossoming that flows over all the plants of a species like a wave of colour, light and warmth. If one travels swiftly southwards for a few days—hours are not enough—the vigilant observer can experience with real intensity how the blossoming-power of different plant-species flows northwards: the sight of a successively more advanced flowering brings it home to him as he passes southwards. This can give one a visual experience not of individual astral bodies but of a group-soul, and here a plant group-soul, which as the season comes

round, pours forth a common astrality over the individual plants
from out of the cosmos, colouring them to our delight and ripening
the fruit with warmth.

We will now have little trouble in understanding how a small child
does not yet have its own individual sheaths but for example a
'maternal astral sheath', as Rudolf Steiner calls it, which flows and
undulates around it. We have not to do here with the astral body of
the child's physical mother but with currents which belong to the
cosmic surroundings. Just as in the womb we are immersed in the
forces of the maternal physical body, so also are we in childhood in
the forces of the cosmos. We can certainly assume that along with the
cosmic astral forces that permeate a child there works into it the
astrality of the environment, of its parents and especially of its mother
—for better or for worse! Of course a child's organs are already
worked through by astrality, but they are not yet so individually
organized as they become from a certain later time on: the sense of
taste, for instance, is not confined to its corresponding organs in the
tongue, for a small child really tastes with its whole body.

That is why a child very much reflects in its own feelings the emotions around it. Who has not seen how the parents' sympathy or
antipathy towards the one or the other acquaintance can be read off
from the children, without these having the least knowledge of what
it is all about? They are simply permeated by the parental emotions.

While the colour-bestowing astrality of plants only descends on
them when the flowers are about to prepare the fruit, the astrality of
the human being, which has previously been weaving a kind of sheath
around him as a child, enters him permanently with sexual maturity
to form his individual astral body. What hitherto enfolded the child
with its cosmic forces is now drawn into the separate organs, being
focussed particularly in the heart. This individualisation of the surrounding astral sheath is a systole of the same kind as the contraction
of the spiritual human being into the physical body at birth: it is the
birth of the astral body, a tightening-together which is a painful experience. Whether the young person is conscious of it or not, his
seniors notice that he grows more serious at this age, subsiding, it
may be, even into melancholy, a *Weltschmerz* that almost wallows
in sheerest pessimism and misanthropy. The understanding parent or
teacher will open up rich, wide-spreading fields of interest to the
sentient body now coming in from its cosmic diastole and so divert

it from brooding over its own plight towards the surrounding world and its problems. The pain felt by the sentient body during its systole can be counteracted in this way, for while it is part of the youthful being's natural development, it should not be left to find its own escape and solace in unprofitable thoughts and actions.

About the twentieth or twenty-first year the ego enters the young person in the same way. Again a systole when seen from the side of the ego, this process is carried through above all by form-bestowing forces that work as far down as the physical body, where for example they bring about a change in the features. They also affect relationships to others and in fact the way of life as a whole.

Once these two members have taken hold of the human body as their own individual vessel, each of them has its own dynamic, its own form of manifestation. An awareness of the subtler differences between astral and ego experiences makes for a more conscious and responsible management of these two members in the interest of the second man and of his shaping.

The joy and sorrow mediated by the astral body are a diastole and systole which is evoked by perceptions of the outer or inner world. These also are themselves transmitted by the astral body, which in external perception reaches out into the world around through the sense-organs and gives us consciousness of it; it responds according to the effect upon itself of what it perceives, with expansion or contraction, diastole or systole, joy or sorrow. We can now understand what Rudolf Steiner meant when he said, 'When we feel joy, the joy of the world experiences itself in us.'[10] The note struck by the outside event lingers on within us, and because it is in our sentient body that it does so, we experience it as feeling, as a stirring of the soul.—Now if the astral body has become cramped through some previous suffering, outside impressions will be obscured as they pass into it; nothing, however beautiful, will leave the slightest impression. The person is out of tune with his surroundings, his sentient body is blocked, it is no longer free to sound, to vibrate sympathetically in harmonious diastole and systole with all the impressions pouring in. The finer and more sensitive in movement the astral body becomes, however, the more delicate the nuances it will respond to in what meets it in the world and other human beings.

The ego enters the organization of the growing human being around the twenty-first year. In his science of man Rudolf Steiner gives an account of each phase of development up to that time, but if we look at these from our present standpoint we can extend and enrich our view of how the spiritual forces of man are at work in us. During a child's third year its ego, the spiritual kernel of man, the central force of his conscious activity, anticipates its entry into possession of its earthly domain; for whereas hitherto its ego has been quite outside the body and in consequence it has been giving itself an outside name just as it does anyone else, it now makes its first preparatory move inwards and begins to call itself 'I'. But the child continues to give itself up completely in a devoted trustfulness to the world around, in the diastole of a soul-expansion into the surroundings, until its ego takes the second anticipatory step inwards in the course of the ninth year. Now quite suddenly it experiences a certain modification of feeling which causes it to pull back somewhat from the environment and to a marked degree upsets its natural acceptance of adult authority. If the parents and teachers do not stand the test imposed by the strengthening ego, the child will have an inner experience that many remember later and that testifies clearly to what is going on. When now with its awakening, more inwardly feeling ego it is not received, should we say, in the right way by the adults around it, it is liable to a kind of shock-condition which issues in the question: 'Who am I? Am I really the child of these parents?' The question is hardly ever expressed as such, but it is no less perturbing for all that, and in some children it engenders great sorrow and a feeling of strangeness that may even culminate in the first thoughts of suicide. Or again, the child's imagination, fed by fairy-tales perhaps, may break forth into a lush growth of fantastic dreams about its own origin. 'Perhaps I am only the foster-child of these people who say they are my parents. Perhaps I am a foundling and really belong to a life altogether more magnificent!' This feeling of being actually a prince or princess in disguise is much more prevalent among children of this age than most parents or teachers imagine; the children keep it as a most closely guarded secret, burying it so deep down in their souls that it often does not emerge again until later in life, only to sink back uncomprehended into oblivion again. It is the first lighting-up of the immortal spirit-centre, which does indeed pass through earthly life in a most humble disguise. If the child is not drawn lovingly into the world of earth, then instead of a first firm stepping down into it there is a startling flashing forth of consciousness within the higher spiritual ego, the shock of which may urge flight from a world too hideous. It is the first tragic moment in the human being's search for his ego. Happy the child whose parents and teachers earn its respect and love, who come before it and its ego's first conscious perception on earth as worthy examples to be followed!

After puberty the ego unceasingly shines gently down upon the surge and struggle of the sentient body, as it claims its place within the human organization and gropes its way out into the world. At this time the aim of education must be to give the ego a nourishment that is worthy of it as it hovers there sun-like above the scene of battle. It is the age-old ego that has journeyed so far already through the streams of time and is now preparing its quarters in this new dwelling, whatever the opposition offered by a warped civilization. Rudolf Steiner took careful and loving account of this struggle in what he recommended for the renewal of education, and in consequence asked from the teachers concerned a very great deal in the way of self-transformation!

How does the ego express itself in the sense of this study? We have already seen that the sentient body lives in the diastole and systole of sleeping and waking, and again of joy and sorrow. Now the fundamental driving-force as well as the essential task of the ego is indicated by Rudolf Steiner in his *Occult Science*[6] where he describes the ego as the 'spark of fire from the Spirits of Form'. These words, bringing home to us that it is form-forces above all which work in the ego, encompass the origin and the goal of human evolution, since this originates in the sun-natured Spirits of Form and it aims at the ego's transformation of astral, etheric and physical bodies into Spirit-Self, Life-Spirit and Spirit-Man. In that process man also spiritualises the physical earth, unforming it we might say out of its mineral state and leading it on to its ultimate fulfilment.

The ego is the starting-point, the source of man's knowledge. We cannot really know anything without concentrating on it with our ego and becoming completely one with it. We cannot really understand another person without giving up our own standpoint and placing ourselves completely within his being. Cold observation without loving sympathy only discloses the other's externalities, mostly indeed his faults. Such a superficial approach does not involve the ego, whose dynamic of knowledge is again a form of active diastole and systole. It is in fact the pre-natal form of knowledge once more, whereby the subject expands into the object to become one with it. This process is based on the ego's essential power of devotion, of selfless love.

This ego-diastole is quite unlike that of the astral body: it is no merely passive reaction to an external or internal impression but an active deed on the part of a man's inmost being. The kind of sympathy that depends on the astral body's satisfaction in the proximity of another gives rise to emotions that flow back and forth between people with group-soul force, and that not in the best sense of the term, as we see for example in mass-meetings. But such emotions will not be associated with any clear knowledge, for the only thing usually observed is what is liked in the other; as for what is not liked, it simply makes the sentient body recoil in antipathy.

When the ego understands another person in active, selfless love, it will recognize not only the other's merits but also his faults, and this without falling into an emotional antipathy. (Such an antipathy can easily become a habit, a constitutional reaction of the sentient body towards the person or thing concerned. There are pathological aversions in some people for example against such things as mice or unfeathered fledglings: these are *idiosyncrasies*—note the affinity of the term to *systole*—that have little enough to do with the ego.)

The knowledge gained through the devotion, through the loving diastole of the ego must be followed by its systole, if a self-formative process is to ensue; in other words by that reflecting upon itself whereby the ego consciously assigns its new-won knowledge to its place in the totality of its own experience. Only the harmonious alternation between the diastole and systole of the ego permits the healthy development of a personality. An incessant outpouring of love will never let it come to a robust self-consciousness, while it will close up within itself if it expands too seldom into the diastole of absorbed attention.

Each one of us in this connection has his own rhythm of diastole and systole. It goes without saying that since the ego and astral body are intimately bound together, the sentient body will swing to the ego's rhythm, accompanying the act of knowledge with the feelings of joy and sorrow, of sympathy and antipathy, which mirror it in the soul. Anyone able to love out of his ego in a healthy life of soul will easily recognize the inner rhythm within it of approach and withdrawal. Having become aware of it, however, one will also have to learn to handle it consciously. The modern soul grows ever more sensitive, so that another's temporary withdrawal can easily be taken negatively as estrangement. As elsewhere, it is only a spiritual understanding of man that enables us to meet the situation at a deeper level. The swing of the pendulum here depends for its period and amplitude, as it were, on the strength of the ego concerned. There are people who radiantly open themselves up to others, lovingly entering into their peculiar qualities—it is like a sudden bursting into flower. But their ego is not strong enough to sustain a long, deep rhythm of breathing, and the next day we may already remark with amazement, perhaps with painful disappointment, that they have completely withdrawn into themselves, as if to blot out all memory of that short-lived effulgence. Dissatisfaction or reproach would here be quite out of place: we have to do with an inwardly tender ego which needs this vehement swing of the pendulum, however brief, to strengthen a self-consciousness which would never be able to maintain itself otherwise; and to help others to maintain their self-consciousness is our highest and holiest duty. When another is in need of distance for his own development's sake, one has then to be capable oneself of a loving withdrawal. Life in a community depends very much on the ability of its members to harmonize their experience of each other, their rhythm of diastole and systole, in an understanding way. This does not mean that they should pull such intimacies to shreds in intellectual discussion: it is rather a matter of silent deeds of consciousness within one's own being.

There are other people capable of such love for the world and for others that they radiate an atmosphere of warmth around them. Their ego-power is strong enough to take the rhythmic movement of diastole and systole quite into themselves, so that for others it is completely overshadowed by the warmth and the calm power of their love.

On the other hand, if the ego cannot expand and enter into whatever calls for its understanding but sticks fast in its systole, then this will become a point of rest instead of passage. Coldness then takes hold of the soul, which in human relationships can intensify to hate. Hate thus represents a bogging-down of the free divine activity of the 'I' within the field of knowledge; a freezing of the soul's warmth-being, of the divine spark of the ego. Hate is the negation of the ego, the surrender of its own proper activity of love. 'Towards you I cannot act out of my divine inner being,' is what we are really saying to someone we hate.

That is why any true striving for inner growth has always aimed first of all at harmonizing the astral body until it can open up to every impression without onesidedly lapsing either into diastolic slackness or systolic cramp. In all these considerations we need to remember that through turning to spiritual beings who were not its own original leaders—through the Luciferic temptation, as it is called—the ego was dislodged as the centre of human activity in knowledge in the widest sense. Its role was usurped by the astral body, which became the origin of the kind of knowledge that 'made us like gods'. As a result, human development has been deeply affected by all that has worked up out of the astral body to befog the ego's true being; for pure ego-power is the pure power of love.

Our aim in developing the ego will therefore be to strengthen and train this power of pure love once more as an organ of knowledge; hate will then dissolve away and also, to the measure of what now lives in us and through our bearing towards them, out of the souls of others; for hate locks out our understanding of others. Rudolf Steiner pointed to the fact that hatred and misunderstanding have grown to such excess among human beings today that, carried into the post-mortal sphere, they can no longer be dissolved by the hierarchies. The result is that something like a spiritual cancer is branching out ever more and more through human civilisation. We should take out of this an admonition to concern ourselves with what actually goes on inwardly as ego and astral experience, so that gradually we learn to form and handle the forces of the second, spiritual man in us.

If we succeed at least in the first steps of this endeavour, we shall not miss the connection between anthroposophy and the work of Goethe. Goethe was the first to discover the law of metamorphosis. His intuitive power of knowledge grasped the primal law of the spiritual forces active in that first border-region where etheric and physical-mineral forces meet in the plant. In spite of his endeavours, however, he was unable to extend his knowledge by way of the animal to the metamorphosis at work in man, because the time was not yet ripe. We are now living in an age when on behalf of mankind Rudolf Steiner was able to take the necessary further step in knowledge: he has shown us how to grasp the metamorphoses taking place in the life of the human soul and thus to raise into consciousness and give further effect to the spiritual laws prevailing in them.

Polarities

The Poles of Form and Life in Man

Up till now our considerations have been based on the twofold division of man's nature into soul and spirit or astral body and ego, and the vessel that receives them, the etheric and physical bodies. The latter constitute the living instrument, the organ for the spiritual man and his deeds on earth, and what we know about sleep and the separative effect of any intensive process of cognition shows that there is only a loose connection between the two.

This human polarity reflects that of the macrocosm. In both cases the opposites concerned develop tensions, the resolution of which gives rise to a third factor. If an investigation of the microcosmic polarity with all its positive and negative effects is to yield at any rate some intimation of the laws it depends on in its whole development, it must also turn to the macrocosmic polarity in which the microcosmic has its primal origin. And as it progresses it will be found that a deeper understanding of the microcosmic phenomenon calls forth a mood of reverence, of piety as Goethe would have said, as the great cosmic archetype is approached.

The effects of these opposites in man are very much in evidence in present-day life and culture, and the ego-man will never resolve the tension he is subjected to until he fully understands it. Let us therefore now look at him in this situation.

It is from the head of man that his formative forces proceed, as can be seen in the embryo, in which the growing and shaping of the whole body take their start from the head. Moreover, in the first seven years it is still the modelling head-forces which play the chief part in the child's development, working from above downwards. Then after the change of teeth they are gradually superseded in their role by forces of an opposite kind: these work from below upwards, and are musical in character. Sculpture is now replaced by music in the configuring processes that work into the growing human being.

The forces issuing from these two poles of man's organization, however, do not only work physiologically but spiritually as well. Thus from the head there proceed spiritual formative forces which as consciousness-creative thinking illuminate the phenomena both of the outer world and the inner life. Man's head-pole is the starting-point for formative forces in the widest sense, for whenever he gives shape to some part of the outer world with his limbs, he does so out of the ideas he has come to in his head. The human head thus gives a basis to the forces that shape the human body and which inwardly we can experience as formative forces of light. They create consciousness, but in doing so they destroy life: the forces of form go together with forces of death. Everyone knows the fatigue that follows strenuous thought; immoderate demands on these forces in child or adult exhaust their vitality as can be seen from the consequent loss of colour from the cheeks. A burly ox of a man with a ruddy face is hardly our idea of a thinker. When at death the mortal forces prevail over the forces of life in the human body, consciousness reaches its climax: the spiritual world is revealed to a dying man in his release from the bounds of physical existence.

From the pole of life, where is concentrated man's organization of limbs and metabolism, there work the opposite forces; stimulated by the nourishment that has been taken in, they stream up life-creative from below, kindling warmth and carrying the forces of will. In creating life, they dull the consciousness. If the life-processes prevail over a man's thought-pole, he lapses into unconsciousness; for if the thyroid gland in the neighbourhood of the larynx is unable to keep the life-forces back, the brain has to do it instead. It is not then able to carry out its own proper function in the activity of thinking, since its consciousness-creative life-restrictive forces have become inadequate.

Just as we associate the head-pole with light, down to our very use of language, the life-pole is related to sound; and as the forces of form strike downwards, so do those of sound flow upwards. A sound has been conjured into every substance as an inner resonance; it is a faint echo of the creative harmony of the world which sounds throughout the universe.

The closer affinity of the life-sphere to sound as compared with the form-sphere may be seen in their respective relationships to speech, to expression through the word. A thoughtful striving after knowledge needs silence, needs to hold back and make inward the forces which would otherwise stream outwards in words. The capacity

to be silent at will is a basic requirement for anyone in occult training. The idea of talkative wisdom is a contradiction in itself.

On the other hand, when feelings arise in the soul, they call urgently for expression. We may be quite sure that when man uttered the
first archetypal tones of speech, he was giving expression not to ideas
but to the feelings which life was arousing in him. Now all our in-
tenser feeling, of amazement, pain and the like, is a living experience
of life and finds expression in those sounds which have in fact to do
with our own life-sphere; in the vowels, that is, which are intimately
related to the bodily organs within it. In the animal world also with
its joy and pain, expression is given in sound to life-feelings that are
untouched by thought. Here, however, it dawns upon us that we have
not to do with the utterance of individual experience but of what,
mightily and mysteriously, stands behind the animal-world as a
whole: the life-principle of the Earth-being itself. Only in man, whose
formative forces enter an individual life-vessel and who carries his
ego in himself and not in a group-soul, does sound give expression
to individual feeling and eventually—in historical as well as personal
development—to individual thought as well. Sound of itself expresses
only feeling: the human word, however, is more than sound, for in it
work the forces of form as well as of life, a synthesis penetrating into
the universe and discoverable within it.

With his head man comes to the creation of enlightening thought, of
well-defined knowledge; with his metabolism he creates life for his
own body and in reproduction the living vessel for a new human being.

A harmonious interplay of the principles of form and of life gives
a life-filled form. Looking at it more closely, we can see that there are
various stages in this interworking of form and matter, of spirit and
life. The spirit enters with shaping force into matter, creating a material form. If it is not strong enough to penetrate so far that it can
go on working within this, then we have to do it maybe with a human
production from which the fashioning spirit has parted company such
as architecture, sculpture or machinery. These in reality are all
thought-forms filled out with matter, which continue in existence
purely as static forms that are without life themselves and cannot
create it.—There is a spirituality above mankind's, however, which
does not abandon matter as soon as it has formed it but re-enters it
ever and again, giving it not only form but inner movement as well:
here the principles of life and form will alternate and so give rise to

rhythm. This can be observed in all the realms of Nature. In man it is in the middle system of the bodily organization that forces which stimulate life and others which create form and so bring about death alternate with each other in a regular time-sequence. The rhythms of blood and breathing are actually brought about by the recurrent interruption of the flow of life by a brief death-process which causes profound changes right down into the chemistry of the body. It is, however, the chemistry of the human body that provides the living, the etheric foundations into which the formative forces of the spirit can enter from above and so create knowledge.

Thus our middle system keeps the balance between the formative, death-bringing forces from above and the life-creating forces from below. If the death-process were to persist longer than the rhythm allows, actual death would ensue. Thus in the rhythmical pauses between breaths and between heart-beats we are really standing every time at the threshold of death without realising it. On the other hand, an excess of life would rob us of the very thing that in the highest sense makes human beings of us: our consciousness by which knowledge is created. For, as we have seen, consciousness is damped down when the head is overflooded with life.

What is the middle, rhythmic man's medium of expression? It is the word. The word, which goes beyond the expression of feelings through mere sound, is in the profoundest sense the expression of the creative collaboration of the upper and lower forces in man. The vehicle, the body of the word is the breath, which comes from man's middle region. Vowels, the sounds manifesting ensouled life-feeling, flow through it; consonants give it shape. Its form—the combination of vowels and consonants—particularly affects the will, whereas its content, what is being said, corresponding to the matter within physical formations, affects man's thinking, modifying its content in turn. Here we have a kind of crossing over, where all may be brought into balance.

Thus we can see in man the polarity of matter and form, of forces of life and of death, of processes that dull and that arouse consciousness. This polarity of the lower and upper forces finds harmonious balance in the middle, the rhythmic system, which is the source of that continuing creation of which among earth-creatures man alone is capable, and which goes forth into the universe as a bestowal of form to which there is no limit. This creation is the Word.

The Upper and the Lower Gods

If we look beyond the external human form, the material substances
within it and the chemical changes in these, and penetrate towards
the deeper creative forces within the body, we arrive at the sublime
polarity which we have been considering: the head forces above,
creating and forming consciousness but consuming, demolishing life,
and the forces of the lower man, creating life, breaking down the
formed nutritive substances coming in from outside and in warmth-
processes changing them into bearers of life. Midway in the human
body these upper and lower forces, as forces of death and of life,
meet in the rhythm of breathing: each in-breathing carries life-
awakening air into the body from out the cosmos just when the death-
forces in the blood reach a maximum. The source of man's life is not
within him but outside in the universe, in that the oxygen-bearing
atmosphere around the body of the earth is in the first place the
vehicle of the earth's astrality, into which play the forces of the stars.
When he breathes in, man is united with the universe and sucks life
in from it, just as in his embryonic stage he 'breathed' his life in from
the maternal organism enclosing him. The difference is that the embryo does not breathe with its middle system but with its lower one,
which governs its metabolism: the blood prepared for it by the maternal organism flows into it through the arteries of the umbilical
cord, and the spent blood flows back through the umbilical vein to be
regenerated by the mother.

Thus man is an embryo of cosmic forces while he breathes on earth.
It can be felt as a deepest mystery of speech that in so many languages
the term for breathing is derived from the same root as the word in
that language—or one related to it generically—that means spirit,
in the sense of that which as the highest principle builds up the physical body. The German *atmen*, to breathe, is related to the Indian
atman, familiar to us from *Atma*, Spirit-man, into which the physical
body will be transformed when it has been completely permeated and
consciously shaped throughout by the ego. In Slavonic we have *od-
dychac*, to breathe; *dyszeć*, to gasp; *duch*, spirit; and *dusza*, soul.
A most significant example is that mysterious passage in St. John's
Gospel, 11.33, about the raising of Lazarus. The original Greek has
ἐνεβριμήσατο τῷ πνεύματι καὶ ἐτάραξεν ἑαυτόν (enebrimēsato tō
etáraxen heautón). Now the root *-bri-* of the first word designates a

process relating to the rushing wind, the panting breath, and blowing in general; the *br-* is present in the English *breathe*, related to the German *brausen*, to bluster, and *Brodem*, vapour, while the Sanskrit *brahma* denotes the supreme cosmic spirit. Unfortunately the usual translation 'He groaned in the spirit, and was troubled', has nothing of all this, and indeed, literally it means: 'He let the spirit rush up within him and he shook in his inner being.' It is the author's way of showing the change that Christ brought about in Himself, letting the spirit rush into His body like a storm-wind, so as to bring Himself out of His usual condition. He let a great change take place in His breath-organism when He called the spirit and the life back into Lazarus' dead body. Something flowed with power from Christ across to His disciple Lazarus, something that brought about the sublime process of resurrection; and it is inwardly related, in a way that human thought can hardly fathom, to these spiritual storm-powers. Such mysteries of life as these are to be found in man, not accessible to the reasoning thought which moves along the surface of things, but revealed only in the creative depths of speech and in the very nature of the word itself. And so it is not only cosmic life-forces which enter into the middle man but also an exalted wisdom which, far beyond our thought as yet, sounds into him by way of its own creation, the word, and impresses its supreme mysteries into our existence.

In the lower man life-bearing matter is prepared, substances that with their earthly character are needed by man only down here on earth, which is also the only place where they can exist. Whereas these are prepared below at man's pole of life, he receives his life-bestowing breath through his middle organisation; it is in a higher sense that life enters here. A deeper study of the physical body and its functions thus brings us to recognise the working of something whose level of being is far above man's, without whose help he could not even exist, let alone come to a fulfilment of his task on earth.

How are these high beings who are at work in the human body revealed to the spirit-eye of man? The physical eye can see only the results, a deeper pondering only the process of their activity.

Let us approach this question first of all with an experience many can have at the present time even if they know nothing of spiritual science and its study of man. Something like the following can often be heard: 'Ever since childhood I have had a dream time and again which has always told the same story, no matter how differently expressed or costumed. I find myself fighting with a raging bull,' or again, 'I have to struggle with an animal like a tiger, a giant cat, . . . a lion'. More rarely altogether will people have dreams about fighting a bird, such as a griffin or an eagle. Those who have begun to harmonize their inner life, though not only such, may have these dreams in a somewhat different form: they may see one or several animals—bull and lion, or an eagle by itself, or all three—while waking up. Sometimes the human face may be woven into the picture of this hierarchical animal-assemblage.

These more or less distorted images, in full dream or when already waking up, are a faint reflection of a spirit-experience the soul can come to in certain circumstances, when simply through sleep or through a severe shock it has parted to some extent from the body and is looking down at it from above. Grossmann, in Albert Steffen's play *Das Viergetier*,[8] has this experience in a particularly impressive way.

The three beasts and the face of the angel or of the man are the first real spiritual experience anyone attains who through inner work is seeking to detach himself from his physical body in full consciousness. He will then see these four hierarchical forms. He may see them in a distorted form or radiant with spiritual beauty and upborne on manifold cherub-wings, depending on how far through his way of life he has spoilt or enhanced what the four divinities thus represented have bestowed on him.

This picture accompanies the whole course of human history, shining forth in it again and again. Let me point to just the best-known and most impressive examples of it. There is a little picture by Raphael in the Galleria Pitti in Florence, showing the four beasts high above a peaceful landscape and in majestic human form carrying the Divine Being; it is usually called *The Vision of Ezekiel*. But anyone who looks up the first chapter of the Book of Ezekiel will realize that Raphael was not painting Ezekiel's vision at all, although they certainly had both had the same experience: the difference in the way the figures are described by the one and painted by the other are too great—as great as that between the Hebrew prophet and the renaissance artist as regards the motive-forces within their souls.—Earlier still in history, at the threshold over which man passed from vision to thought, we come to the sphinx. This combination of the four zodiacal beasts was worshipped by the Egyptians, feared by the Greeks, and hurled into the abyss by Oedipus when he had solved her riddle. The task of the Greek was to concentrate his ether-body so as to transform vision into thought. In this process the sphinx as a picture of an obsolete mode of experience could now only oppress him as the essential pain of questioning. The sight of her was devastating, but he sought a solution and found it.

These figures accompanying mankind through the ages, what are they? Rudolf Steiner enabled us to understand what once came with such power before the inner eye. He described how early in human evolution the newly-forming physical body of man was not present in its physical-mineral state. On Ancient Saturn it took shape as a body of warmth that followed physical laws; on Ancient Sun its warmth was penetrated by air, and on Ancient Moon its warmth and air by water. Only on the earth did mineral substance began to enter it at last. This process was so gradual, however, that the highest divine beings could form it before it really materialized and hardened. In ancient Lemuria, powers belonging to the highest hierarchical regions rose out of the depths to build the human body, such as it was then, into the form of a bull; moreover, the human souls beheld these beings themselves in bull-form. In the early Atlantean periods other hierarchies appeared and, seen in lion-form, transformed the human body into that shape also. In late Atlantis eagle-forces flowed down from cosmic heights with formative power. Finally, though much later, this multiform human body was imbued with the ego and so given the human countenance.

Here we can see at work the hierarchical beings who formed the human body. The real form of the human body as seen spiritually looks nothing like what we see in our ordinary consciousness. If a soul perceives the spiritual aspect of the physical body while free of it during sleep, or while continuing to be thus free when waking up or through having enlarged its sheaths through training, it will see it in the form of the four 'beasts', of the powers of the zodiac that shaped it and still give it life. It is the form of the throne, that is, the physical vessel, of the Son of Man, which is what is beheld in the vision of Ezekiel and the picture of Raphael. All the mythological and religious pictures mentioned above contain the experiences of individual seers who penetrated to the spiritual vision of the physical human body.

Let us note that in the course of history it was in a certain sequence that these exalted beings were worshipped as holding sway over the religious life. The earliest cultures venerated the bull or cow as the power that bore the forces of life. This can be proved many times over out of ancient myths and documentary records, including those of the ancient Persian period. From even as late as the third post-Atlantean period there are pictures of Isis with cow-horns. Somewhat later, in Assyrian and Babylonian art, the lion begins to predominate, for example at the Ishtar Gate of Babylon. The lion-drawn carriage of the mother of the gods is an important element in ritual as far as Asia Minor. This Asiatic priestly culture then gives way to the war-like Greeks with their kings who could think and were full of guile, and worshipped Zeus who was himself king of gods and men. The eagle is the symbol of this new regent of the world, itself representing the formative wisdom of the head-powers on a cosmic scale. Eagles bring wisdom to Zeus and the knowledge of all that happens on earth—a service also done for Odin by the ravens about his head.

We are tracing here a quite definite line of development. The history of religion shows that early man was intimately united with the forces of life and accordingly worshipped those powers of life above all who as the creative, fertile gods he knew held sway in the life-bearing depths of the earth and in the fertile waters of the ocean. They were to him the great, even the supreme gods, gods who create life but who also dissolve life's earthly forms in death to allow new life to follow. Ancient humanity associated the highest, life-creating powers with the dark depths of night from which in times long past the forces arose which gave a bull-form to the body of man. Life and love were holy above all to early man as the supreme creative powers. Reverence brought trembling upon him when he turned to them in worship or came near where their forces were at work.

Much later religions embraced the worship of the powers of wisdom, of the gods who promoted thought. Zeus, who cast the old gods into the bowels of the earth, first married Metis, the goddess of contemplative cosmic wisdom, who came from this ancient line of gods herself. Hers should have been the destiny to beget the goddess of wisdom who was to shape the world, but Zeus deceived her. Having persuaded her to change into a fly, he swallowed her and could now himself give birth to Athene out of his head: Athene, the thought-weaving goddess who taught mankind moral independence and clear, controlled thinking. These wise gods, who could be right crafty as

well, were full of light, flooding the world with brightness. In the
light of their thoughts mankind developed a mode of thinking that
more and more turned to earthly reality, while the mysterious divine,
dark depths of life with their ancient gods sank into oblivion. As he
went down into the material world he lost all experience of them and
was led along other ways into the religious life.

Rudolf Steiner's teaching reveals in this line of religious development the reflection of great cosmic processes and polarities. The gods
of the oldest, most powerful hierarchies are those whose will can
work directly into the earth's very substance. This is the highest
hierarchy, worshipped as the gods of the world-depths who in the
fashioning of the earth formed and still form its substances. The
ancient Romans called them *di inferi*, the lower gods, the earliest
Asiatic and Greek religions 'the great gods', the *kabeiroi*.

Such exalted beings, when they think, do not produce the vague
impermanent phantoms of our kind of thought: the thoughts of these
oldest and mightiest gods were gods again, whose range of power,
however, did not extend into physical matter but only to that of the
soul, of human knowledge. These upper gods, *di superi*, were not
bearers of life but of light-filled wisdom. The popular Greek religion
that has come down to us through Homer hardly reached beyond
these upper gods; the forms of the highest, most ancient divinities
were glimpsed only as through a thick veil.

We find this polarity in the respective forms of ancient worship.
The light-bearing upper gods were worshipped in rites which had to
do with light, with sacrificial fire. Originally the priests cut out a grass
rectangle and built the earth up towards the down-streaming light:
this was the primitive altar—a term which comes from the Latin
altus, high, so that *altare* was the high place. On this altar the priest
lit the flame, which together with the words of prayer rose up towards
the lofty regions of the light and its divine guardians.

In the worship of the lower gods an approach to their realm was
made again in the way the cult was ordered: the altar now was built
downwards instead of upwards as a more or less regular square hole
in the earth in the shape, that is, of an altar, such as can still be found
in old temple ruins in Greece and Asia Minor. It was closed by a
decorated cover, but the bottom and sometimes also the sides were
left as bare, living earth: for the offering here was not of fire that with
its light flames upwards to the heights of wisdom, but the warm, life-

bearing blood of an animal that flowed down to the life-giving powers in the depths. Thus there were two kinds of altar, the one raised up, the other hollowed out of the earth like a grave, whereon as tables of offering the various divine hierarchies were given back by men that which was their due.

This polarity of the upper and the lower gods was observed in rituals that survived for a long time, and in some cases have done so to this day. For example, in the centre of a Roman Catholic altar-top there is still always an almost closed-over, small, level hollow containing relics, bones indeed of some saint revered as a representative of Christendom. It is a late, hardly conscious survival from early Christian times of the profound knowledge that Christ's table of offering must unite the altar and the grave in itself because Christ, the cosmic Logos, unites all the heights and depths in Himself.

The upper and the lower gods are the mighty beings who together build up the human body. When the lower gods had to make way for the worship of the upper gods because the ever more deeply incarnating human spirit could no longer understand their mysteries, man also lost the knowledge and understanding of the processes going on within the life-pole of his own body. He developed the wisdom born of thought, so that his culture and religion were more and more governed by the head. As the real knowledge of the gods and of the earth gradually waned, abstract knowledge remained and took its place in the estimation of man, and it is still supreme today. The powers of life are still there; they are at work indeed as always, but their working no longer calls forth the ancient religious awe. The profanation it has suffered is complete.

As men lost their old understanding and purity of feeling, they could no longer find their way to the divinities of the depths; a fearful decline set in within the cultic life, showing itself within certain circles in orgiastic frenzies and the like. Instead of the pure and exalted divinities of life, demonic entities presided at the desecrated altars, whilst the ancient wisdom faded away into mere regulation and formalized doctrine. At this crucial moment an exalted being, Himself originating in the middle region, in the sun, the centre of the cosmic system, was breathed out of the heights into mankind and into the very body of the earth herself: Christ, the Cosmic Word, was incarnated. When the great cosmic breath had itself come close to the point of death for mankind and the earth, this Being came out of

the universe to heal the cosmic polarities of which our bodies are a
smaller image.

Thus man and his word are in all reality an image of exalted cosmic
processes. Indifference to the middle realm in all things has sundered
the polarities of thinking and living, of the upper and lower man,
and brought the world to its present pass. The modern sickness can
be healed only if ever more consciously we again make our own a
knowledge of these world-polarities in their highest, most spiritual
sense, for then we shall find once more the middle realm in its reality.

Harmonizing the Opposites

How does the polarity of forces at work in life and knowledge show
itself in the world today? In no sense have they come to harmony in
the ordinary human being, nor in fact can they do so as long as the
education of children stays as it is. This still concerns itself primarily
with knowledge, with the head-pole, since it is knowledge that modern
society, and consequently the parents within it, demands; knowledge
after all passes for power today. But education of this sort does
nothing for the pole of the will. It happens often enough that the
product of its methods find himself at sea in actual life, since with
all the knowledge and training he has acquired he has little idea of
what in the chaos of modern conditions he should set his will to
achieve. The knowledge he needs for this is of another kind altogether,
one able at any given moment to rise up out of the depths of the self,
out of a level of the soul where it is not simply stored up on its own
but where it lives in closest union with the powers of will. With only
a one-sided education behind them many people today are easily
pulled into this or that group or party whose common will-sphere is
dominated by the forcefulness of a single individual. Those who break
free again through some independence of mind are the exceptions,
and even most of these are moved by an indeterminate feeling, however deep, of unsatisfied ideals.

Today's education, outcome as it is of a materialistic view of man,
is at best a help in the accumulation of knowledge; it is nothing of
the kind in the taking hold of the will with the conscious ego. Many
adults who sense as a result that there is something lacking in their
own make-up and cast about for what can put this right, come to the
question: 'How can I train my will?' Or it can be, more egoistically:
'How can I get on in life?'

Modern civilization does provide an answer to this question, but in a very one-sided fashion. Recognizing the limbs as the instruments of the will, it seeks a training for them in sport, and since this strengthens the body and develops a certain presence of mind it does of course contribute to the education of the will. As it only does so from the bodily, the physical-material side, however, it solves no more than a fraction of the problem: it offers nothing towards that harmonization of forces of which the modern soul and spirit as well as the body are in such pressing need.

Through such modern practices the two poles of human nature are split apart as hardly ever before in history. Whilst immense stress is laid on developing the head-pole in the direction of a sheerly abstract thinking, the forces at the pole of life are channelled for the most part into external bodily activity; for so many today it is the skilled man of brawn who counts as hero, whether on the football-field or in the boxing-ring.

Now since the last century man has come to concentrate his attention particularly on the material world, and rightly so: after all, it was his task, historically speaking, to establish his mastery over it. He turned all his thought therefore to the processes that go on within the physical-mineral world, and in consequence he developed a type of knowledge that deals only with the material, with what is dead. He has done so certainly in masterly fashion and used it in his various technologies to give to matter the forms devised by his own thought and so to satisfy his outer needs and desires. But this kind of thinking does not open up the world of life; human ingenuity comes to a stop before it, unable in it to unfold any creative ability whatsoever. Here it has no trace of mastery: all the efforts on the part of science to penetrate the mystery of life have only taught man an ever greater perfection in producing death. The art of destruction has reached a climax in all fields of human society. Moreover, the will to kill, the claim even of the right to kill will grow in time beyond all bounds. War-technicians think out more and more ingenious methods of destroying life. 'Progressive' personalities urge the right to do away with human beings they consider morally or physically inferior, or who enter life unwanted. These are the excrescences our modern head-knowledge cannot but breed: it is confined by its very nature to the lifeless, and what it produces inevitably corresponds to what it knows.

As a result of this type of thinking, the forces of life, of the opposite pole in man, once revered as the realm of supreme spirit-beings, have lost all connection for science with antyhing spiritual. They have been desecrated by a merely intellectual inquiry which only finds parallels in them to the animal. In consequence its forces remain beyond human reach not to mention human control so long as the will is not as it were sublimed so as to direct its activity to the living spirit. What is done instead is to make the same kind of technical approach to the living human being as has led to such success with bridges, railways and veritable masterpieces in machine-invention of every kind. It is significant that it is just in the realm of surgery, where the kind of thinking used comes its nearest to the living body, that the achievement has been so impressive. It is significant also from our present point of view that the medical engineers of today seek the management of the life-forces in man not out of any higher insight but through the study of how they function in the animal. They count it as their latest triumph (1935) that they can now insert animal glands into the human body in order to renew and prolong its life. Rudolf Steiner has opened up far-reaching possibilities for the modern human spirit to work ever more consciously, through ways of self-training not yet generally recognised, into the actual realm of these forces, but the direction still persisted in today leads not into this realm of the superhuman and divine but into that of the subhuman and the animal.

Anyone who takes all this into account must see the present moral decline only as the natural result of this unbalanced development. Man has consigned himself solely to matter, placing all his trust in it, with the consequence that he can understand and consciously use only the bodily part of himself with its two polar urges of knowledge and life.

But this does not engage his whole self. There lives in him a second man, who first hovers around and envelops the infant and then gradually moves inwards until he completely unites with the physical organs at puberty. In the chapter 'The Second Man in Us' we saw how the second man enters the physical body from above, as it were head first, so that the eagle-forces of his head, of his thinking, unite with the bull-forces, the will-forces, of the lower physical man and vice versa.

What is then the practical consequence of bringing the second man alive in ourselves and cultivating through him our endeavours towards the spirit? If the will-force of the second man, the man of soul and spirit, becomes active in the physical head, then will begins to work in the thinking and dead thinking to be transformed into one that touches, that reaches out like a limb into the surroundings. This kind of thinking embraces more than the impressions that approach and enter our senses of themselves: it can take the initiative and search for the unknown, it comes gradually to an investigation of the spirit. It is really so; activated by the will, thinking gradually learns to stretch out like a seeking hand, not into the physical but into the spiritual environment. The spiritual organs, now alive and mobile, will touch and recognize spiritual realities. Anyone awakened in his thinking can touch with his thoughts and reach out in full consciousness towards what surges round him in the spiritual light. With the increased strength of his thinking he attains the stage of Imagination, and the pictures he sees do not just flow around him like a panorama —he learns to enter into them, with the strength of the limbs, as it were, of his second man; he can deliberately make his way into any one of them, whereupon all the others flooding in on him disappear, and from his place of vantage he learns to move within this picture-world. What was an arbitrary upwelling of pictures he now can follow in any particular direction; penetrating into it instead of letting it merely flow past him, he learns to find his bearings in this new world as a searcher for truth.

On the other hand, an individual who has thus learnt to activate the knowledge-pole of the second man within him will have no wish to give his will-forces that merely instinctive outlet through the body to which reference has already been made. He will learn to use them as an instrument of knowledge, as a means of entering into the phenomena of the world around him in quest of their inmost nature. He will learn to look inside—*intueri* in Latin—those forms of existence and states of life that evade the exterior view of physical knowledge. Intuition, to use Rudolf Steiner's term for the exact mode of cognition which employs the will as knowledge-force, becomes possible when the knowledge-pole of the second man in us shines through our first man's pole of will.

This description by no means contradicts what Rudolf Steiner often said: 'Carry thinking into willing—willing into thinking.' With the second man becoming more active in us, a livelier connection is set up between thinking and willing, which as polarities no longer veer away from each other with such destructive results. Ordinary thinking

and willing will themselves be balanced by what now flows back
and forth between them, whereas in one who has gone through a
spiritual training and has attained a certain higher stage of perfection, pure thinking will become pure willing, as Rudolf Steiner put it
in his *Youth Course.*[5]

Only by grasping the nature of the second man in this way can the
polarities be harmonized that are splitting man increasingly apart in
our time. All abstract appeals to morality, all measures oblivious of
the spirituality in man which anthroposophical spiritual science has
newly brought to light, can heal nothing of the chaos now besetting
mankind. But activation of the second man must begin from within
one's own ego. In one's own ego is the only source of help. This must
intervene with its formative activity by consciously turning to the
second man. Of course every individual attempting this will need the
basic knowledge that will yield him a true picture of the human being.
That is why the ego-power is so centrally important in the present
phase of human evolution. It is in man's 'I' that the healer and saviour
is to be found.

It will have been noticed that although the poles of head and will in
the second man coincide with their respective physical opposites, the
two middle zones work together. This is in fact the middle human
being's particular significance, and it is why many old representa-
tions, particularly those of the Rosicrucian alchemists, actually show
two lions to portray the middle man; they are frequently in two
colours also, and we find them referred to as the red and the green
lion. Sometimes one is devouring the other, which indicates that the
earthly power within the middle sphere must let itself be devoured by
what corresponds to it in the second man. Then human feeling will
become cosmic feeling and grow beyond the egoistic personality's
narrow limits. Thus as was said in chapter III, we have:—

Physical man	*The second man*
Eagle	Bull
Lion	Lion
Bull	Eagle (Scorpion)

This can explain why the path of feeling is the one leading more immediately into the spirit: for if the soul's power of feeling strives to
penetrate upwards into the spirit, it can stay within its own realm,

unhindered by any conflicting polarities. Enhancement, not polarity, is what is at work along this path.

The middle, the heart-region of man was always pictured as that of the sun, which is indeed macrocosmically the centre of the planetary system. We have already seen that a higher power of wisdom and a higher power of life flow into the middle man in his breath. It is just here that these forces enter into him from out of the universe. It was always known in ancient times that the Being eventually called Christ was the highest Sun-Spirit and that He was gradually coming closer to the earth. This gives many a passage in St. John's Gospel a special meaning, as for example at the very beginning, where the cosmic Word is described: 'In him was life . . . and the life was the light of men,' or when Christ says, 'I am the light of the world,' and 'I am the life.' Christ unites in Himself these two cosmic polar opposites: that is why He is the Healer and Saviour. He is that power of the middle which modern man must take up into himself as he searches for remedy in a disintegrating world.

In ancient schools of inner training men were always exhorted to seek the sun. 'See the sun at the hour of midnight,' was the admonition of the hierophant to his pupil. The sun is the macrocosmic aspect of the Christ-Spirit. In our present culture we have completely lost this aspect: Christ has come to be regarded as a divine being quite apart from the universe, while many leading theologians have even stripped all divinity off Him, saying He is just the simple man of Nazareth!

Humanity now stands before the task of finding Christ the Sun-Spirit again; not through an abstract thinking alone but in real experience. Then we will gradually take into ourselves again the Christ in His cosmic aspect. The Christ-Sun is more than simply a picture: it is the macrocosmic reality of which our middle heart-man, bound up as we have seen with the cosmos, is the image. In this sense, 'to seek the sun' means to seek cosmic reality, to strive towards a conscious experience of the forces working into our middle sphere from out the cosmos. This centre of cosmic light and life in man needs to be enlivened so as to give it sovereignty over the polar opposites within him. This was always the aim of man's spiritual teachers. There was one centre of initiation, for example, that was particularly concerned with kindling in its pupils an understanding of their cosmic origin: it was in ancient Samothrace, where in the temple one of the

Kabiri figures,* the Sun God, representing the Christ that was to come, was given the central position in the holy of holies. The one-sidedness in the head-pole of the pupil was counteracted through inner training by a strengthening of the middle forces. The Samo-thracian priests called this the raising of the heart into the head. Along this inner path the middle man was strengthened: the inner sun began to shine through the power of knowledge.

At a later period we find Christian schooling, in the more particular sense, likewise stressing the training of the feeling-life. Those following this path sought to experience Christ's own passion step by step as if they were going through all His suffering themselves. At a still later stage, the alchemists spoke of producing gold; what they really did was to prepare the middle man to become an organ for spiritual perception—they wanted to learn to create gold, the sun-metal, in themselves.

The picture of the middle heart-man as the cosmic sun is full of such mighty formative forces that their range far exceeds the scope of the individual. It is unthinkable that such a powerful picture, accompanying man's strivings since the very beginning, should not also have some special, essential meaning for the future. And indeed, Rudolf Steiner tells us that the goal of earthly evolution is the sun: in the distant future the earth itself is to become the sun of a new cosmic system.

This brings together all that we have hitherto been considering: the goal of our planet earth is to become a sun. The Spirit of the present sun has already united Himself with the body of the earth through His sacrifice on the cross, and man as an image of the macrocosm is one with this just through his middle being of heart and breath, through his breathing in of light and strength, of wisdom and life. His ego, his warmth-entity, is a spark from the forming-force of the Sun-spirits, and as we have seen, from ancient times till now he has been led through spiritual guidance along a central inner path to seek the sun. From this we may learn what the task of man actually is: amongst earthly denizens he is the bearer of the highest spirituality, and is called on as thinking being to harmonize the polar opposites within himself, and thus make towards that sun-form within, in full consciousness of the spirit and in inner experience, which in outer reality the earth as a whole will one day achieve. The goal of the earth, to become a sun, is to be anticipated and, as it were, prefigured in man's spiritual development.

The centre-bridge we set up between the polarities within us is thus not only a means to our own inner peace and harmony: we not only win such a purely personal benefit but also, objectively speaking and however modestly, help onward the earth-being itself in its own development. First as idea in thinking, then practically in the inner development of the microcosm of man, we begin to realise the future configuration of the macrocosm as a whole.

The present antithesis of the poles in man is the work of the two retarding spirits who spare no effort to prevent this future coming to pass. The one would have all spirituality hardened into matter, the other lead man away from his world-tasks through using his vital creative powers to satisfy his own narrowly egoistic desires. By taking hold of the second man in ourselves we help to heal, to reconcile these polarities in the way our time so urgently needs. We collaborate in the cosmic enterprise of the earth's becoming a sun, we help that the Sun-Spirit transforms the earth-planet even down to its physical formation, into His own body. Just as this great secret of the earth's development was once entrusted to Christ's disciples in the words: 'Whosoever eats my bread, treads my body with his feet,' meaning the earth-body of the Sun-Spirit, so we today receive it in an old mystery-saying which Rudolf Steiner brought to life again in a Christmas verse,* and illuminated with the new light of anthroposophical knowledge:

In darkness living,
Create a sun!

Reminiscence of Rudolf Steiner

To meet a great spirit is like witnessing the rise of an incomparable star. Light from a higher source shines out across the dark fringe of the horizon. And as men of old saw in such stars the impending fulfilment of past prophecies, so today the one whose soul opens in devotion at such a meeting will feel: Through this being light rays into my life from out of spirit-worlds; in it the past becomes transparent, the future itself more distinct.

This was my experience whenever I met Rudolf Steiner. My life found its direction: threads of destiny became visible, linking what had been to what was to come.

Let me describe one of these meetings: it was on the evening of the 26 February 1922. The hall in the Dornach *Schreinerei* was crowded with an expectant audience. Dr. Steiner entered and began to speak with someone. Listening in friendliest sympathy, he bent his head towards the speaker while inclining his face and gaze upwards. His sensitive profile stood out against the light-blue stage-curtain, shedding gentleness and wisdom like a silver light. I had never seen such beauty before.

But at that moment a countenance, a mask with pain-filled features rose up within me. Memories awoke: a girl of about eighteen, waiting on the world around her with an inner stillness; weighty experiences took on form as pictures and plastic forms. To give shape to everything was really beyond her, but she carried it within herself as her dialogue with a life whose riddles were legion and into which her way was leading her ever more deeply.

One thing I found particularly painful at that time, and that was my first awareness of how people near to me were meeting their old age. Resignation was something which hitherto I had known nothing of at all: only development, only the future had existed in my estimation, both for myself and others. It was something altogether new for me to see people no longer reckoning with any further progress in

101

themselves, simply going downhill as they let old age take over. It was an aging that did not lead into the light; death had laid its hand heavily on their shoulders, forcing their gaze towards the grave. Weariness oozed from them and a depressing obtuseness towards everything unfamiliar. I found it painful in the extreme.

But I heard it cried out within me: This is not the way to grow old! Then longing created in me the contrary picture: a wonderfully fine and sensitive face in which a life's experience had become inner light, gently radiant throughout the whole being, breathing wisdom and flowing out in love.

But first of all another head took shape under my hands. It was that mask, whose features were lined with suffering. It was not death it spoke of but dying life that tainted the air around it.

There lived on inside me, however, the longing for the other picture, of the old man resplendent with light. It lived in me, but my hands could not form it.

Life led me further; I saw new faces, and out of how many of them did there show the features of the mask, out of tired old faces and despairing youthful ones! But I could not succeed in shaping the other head.

And now, on the 26 February 1922 I saw what I had been looking for: the countenance I had longed to behold was there before me, its goodness full of wisdom, its love full of understanding.

Before such beauty of spirit, the mask vanished. I visited Dr. Steiner in his Studio the next morning, and when he there showed me the great statue carved in wood, he also made clear to me how I could come to myself. He gave me new courage and fresh enthusiasm for my work. I had met a great spirit, a star shining in the darkness and showing me the way to go.

References

[1] RUDOLF STEINER, *Knowledge of the Higher Worlds: How is it Achieved?* (London, 1969)

[2] RUDOLF STEINER, *Die Erkenntnisaufgabe der Jugend* (Dornach 1957)

[3] RUDOLF STEINER, *Geisteswissenschaft als Erkenntnis der Grundimpulse sozialer Gestaltung*, lecture of 11.9.1920 (complete edition No. 199, Dornach 1967)

[4] RUDOLF STEINER, *The Philosophy of Freedom* (London, 1964)

[5] RUDOLF STEINER, *The Younger Generation* (New York, 1967)

[6] RUDOLF STEINER, *Occult Science—An Outline* (new translation, London 1963)

[7] RUDOLF STEINER, *Karmic Relationships*, lecture 13, vol. V (London, 1966)

[8] ALBERT STEFFEN, *Das Viergetier* (Dornach, 1959)

[9] RUDOLF STEINER, 12th lecture in *The Gospel of St. John* (New York, 1973)

[10] RUDOLF STEINER, *A Road to Self-Knowledge* (London, 1976)

Notes

Page 2

* Andrzej Towiański (1799–1878) was one of those who emigrated from the part of Poland under Russian dominion and came as representatives of Polish spiritual life to the West.

Page 3

* Steiner speaks at length about Dilthey in the chapter 'Modern Man and his World Conception' in *The Riddles of Philosophy* (New York, 1973)

Page 5

* See the author's essay in *Rudolf Steiner: Recollections by Some of his Pupils* (London, 1958)

Page 17

* Lecture of 21.6.1923 in *Die menschliche Seele in ihrem Zusammenhang mit göttlich-geistigen Individualitäten* (complete edition No. 224, Dornach 1966)

Page 20

* 9th lecture in *True and False Paths in Spiritual Investigation* (London, 1969)

Page 22

* The Wandervogel movement of the first decades of this century.

Page 26

* Lecture of 10.12.1917 in *Geschichtliche Notwendigkeit und Freiheit* (complete edition No. 179, Dornach 1965)

Page 30

* Rudolf Steiner, 3rd lecture in *Karmic Relationships*, vol. III (London, 1957)

Page 31

* Johann Wolfgang von Goethe, *Fairy Tale of the Green Snake and the Beautiful Lily*, translated by Thomas Carlyle

Page 38

* To a certain extent *The Younger Generation*[5]—also known as the *Youth Course* —can be regarded as a metamorphosis of *The Philosophy of Freedom* such as Rudolf Steiner wanted to give to younger people in order to lead them to living thinking, to an 'artistic' experience of the world; in other words, to seeing in pictures.

Page 40

* Fra Angelico's pictures offer us an example of such delicacy in colouring. When instead of scenes from the life of Christ it is the spiritual form of Christ or of the Madonna he is painting, he lets both of them appear in an iridescent white so that they emerge from the background of gold in a breath-like gentleness of colour. We may imagine that such are the colours in which the picture-experiences mentioned come before the spiritual eye.

Page 42

* Pausanias, *Description of Greece*, Book 9, Chapter 39

Page 48

* See Rudolf Steiner, *The Gospel of St. John in Relation to the other three Gospels* (London 1968)

** King James's translators did no better (translators' note)

Page 49

* The Greek term *pneuma* designated the air, especially the air in movement and enlivened by the spirit. The sole meaning 'spirit' did not originate until later, when sensible and supersensible experience had begun to fall apart for human consciousness.

Page 50

* The Greek term εγτολή (entole), usually translated as 'commandment', contains the root τελ (tel) meaning 'end', 'goal', 'aim', 'initiation'.

Page 53

* The term *devachan* denotes in Spiritual Science the actual spirit-world above the etheric and astral cosmic regions.

Page 55

* Lecture of 2.12.1923 in *Mystery Knowledge and Mystery Centres* (London,1973)

Page 56

* Just as physical nature is made up of the four elements of earth, water, air and fire, so the ether world has four different modes of activity, namely those of the warmth-ether, light-ether, sound-ether and life-ether.

Page 69

* Lecture of 17.2. 1922 in *Alte und neue Einweihungsmethoden* (complete edition No. 210, Dornach 1967)

Page 100

* Rudolf Steiner, lecture of 21.12.1923 in *Mysteriengestaltungen* (complete edition No. 232, Dornach 1958)

Page 101

* In *Wahrspruchworte* (complete edition No. 40, Dornach 1969)